To The Teacher

This Activity Book is designed to accompany *Human Heritage: A World History*. Using a chapter/unit approach, it consists of student activities based on the 39 chapters and 12 units of the text. Each student activity reinforces text materials, or adds interesting new elements to what has already been learned. The activities are presented in the form of map exercises, fill-in paragraphs, original writing activities, charts, vocabulary word scramblers, and crossword puzzles.

Each chapter section consists of a standard "Focus on Ideas" activity to reinforce students' knowledge of the chapter content. A vocabulary activity serves as a recall exercise to ensure understanding of key terms. Skill activities provide reinforcement through both student application of text information and practice in skill application, and also offer creative opportunities.

Each unit section consists of a geography activity which emphasizes one of the five themes of geography: place, location, region, movement, and human/environmental interaction. This strengthens the geography-history connection for students. A second activity reviews the unit's Around the World feature. This offers students additional opportunities to investigate different world cultures.

To The Student

This Activity Book has been designed for use with *Human Heritage: A World History.* Its purpose is to help you develop an understanding of the distant and not-so-distant past. It reinforces your knowledge of textbook information and broadens your understanding of world history and the different people who have been part of it beyond that provided by the textbook. Each chapter and unit in the text has a corresponding chapter and unit in the Activity Book. After careful reading and study of the text, you should complete the Activity Book exercises as assigned by your teacher.

Chapters and units generally deal with a major civilization or time period. You will be asked to define vocabulary words; identify important names, dates, and places; locate specific geographic locations; and answer questions that relate to world history. You will also have the opportunity to be creative in doing many of these activities. It is important that you have an understanding of the points covered in each chapter and unit before moving to the next one.

Each activity contains complete directions. Space is provided for your answers to each question. You will want to think carefully about your answers before you begin to write. In addition to your textbook and class notes, the completed Activity Book exercise will be helpful to you in preparing for tests.

Table of Contents

Geography and History

FOCUS ON IDEAS

Fill in each blank to form a summary of Chapter 1 by choosing the proper term from the words listed below.

artifacts	erosion	location	plateaus
carbon 14	geography	minerals	pressure
climate	landforms	movement	regions
currents	latitude	nonrenewable	waterways

Ever since people have been on earth, _____ has influenced how and where people have lived. Geographers use five themes to explain what a place is like and why it is like that. These themes are _____, place, human/environmental interaction, _____, and _____. Some 30 percent of the earth's surface is made up of _____that include four major shapes: hills, mountains, plains, and _____, or raised areas of flat or nearly flat land. _____ and heat change the earth's surface from within. Outside sources like the movement of tectonic plates and _____, or changes forced by wind, water, and ice, constantly alter the earth's crust. About 70 percent of the earth's surface is made up of _____, or oceans, rivers, seas, and lakes.

The pattern of weather over a period of years in one place is called _____. This is influenced by the sun, large bodies of water, altitude, winds, and ocean _____, or water flowing in a steady, onward motion. Three climate zones based on _____ are the tropical, temperate, and polar zones.

Materials found in nature, or natural resources, consist of air, water, sunlight, fossil fuels, forests, animal life, and _____, or nonliving substances found beneath the earth's surface. People have become more aware of making better use of the earth, especially with nonreplaceable resources, or _____ resources.

Scientists called archaeologists study _____, or items made by ancient people, to learn how they lived. A method that determines how old an item is, measures the remaining amount of _____, a radioactive element contained in all living things.

USING VOCABULARY

From the definitions given, find the proper term to fill in the missing letters of each line. Then, using the numbered letters from each term, fill in the missing letters for the mystery word and write its definition on the line provided. Terms to use are at the end of the activity.

A. __ __ __ __ __ __ __ __   __ __ __ __   area that receives most direct rays of sun
   1   5 9 7 8   6 2

__ __ __ __ __   made up of a hot, molten rock
  11   12 10 13

__ __ __ __   earth's thin outer layer
3   14 4

__ __ __ __ __ __ __ __   _____
1 2 3 4 5 6 7 8

__ __ __ __ __ __
9 10 11 12 13 14

B. __ __ __ __ __ __ __   material found in nature
20   26 2

__ __ __ __ __ __ __ __
  6   28

__ __ __ __ __ __ __ __ __   different shapes of the earth's surface
18 4 29   3

__ __ __ __ __ __ __ __   water flowing in a steady motion
25   14 5

__ __ __ __ __ __ __ __   study of remains of past human life
  10 1 11

__ __ __ __ __ __   height above sea level
  8   9   7

__ __ __ __ __ __ __ __ __ __   usually cold in winter and warm in summer
16 13   24 22   15

__ __ __ __ __ __ __ __ __   things made by ancient people
17   19   21

__ __ __ __ __ __   sections of the world
23   27 12

__ __ __ __ __ __ __ __ __ __ __ __ __ __ __ __ __ __
1 2 3 4 5   6 7 8 9 10 11 12 13 14 15 16 17 18

__ __ __ __ __ __ __ __ __ __ __   _____
19 20 21 22 23 24 25 26 27 28 29   _____

(continued)

C. $\_\ \_\ \_\ \_\ \_\ \_\ \_$
$\hspace{4.5cm} 2\ \ 6$

$\overline{13}\ \ \overline{11}\ \ \_\ \ \overline{7}\ \ \overline{15}$

$\overline{1}\ \ \_\ \ \_\ \ \_\ \ \overline{10}\ \ \overline{4}$

$\_\ \ \overline{3}\ \ \overline{9}\ \ \_\ \ \_\ \ \_\ \ \_\ \ \_\ \ \_\ \ \_\ \ \_$

$\_\ \ \_\ \ \_\ \ \_\ \ \overline{5}\ \ \_\ \ \overline{8}\ \ \_\ \ \_\ \ \_\ \ \_\ \ \overline{12}$

$\_\ \ \_\ \ \_\ \ \overline{14}\ \ \_\ \ \_\ \ \_\ \ \_\ \ \_\ \ \_$

$\overline{1}\ \overline{2}\ \overline{3}\ \overline{4}\ \overline{5}\ \overline{6}\ \overline{7}\ \overline{8}\ \overline{9}\ \overline{10}\ \overline{11}$

$\overline{12}\ \overline{13}\ \overline{14}\ \overline{15}\ \overline{16}$

process that reshapes the earth's surface

changes in land's height

pattern of weather in one place over several years

one who studies the origin of humans

usually blows from one direction

a river and all streams that flow into it

_____

_____

Terms to Use: anthropologist, archaeology, artifacts, climate, crust, currents, elevation, erosion, landforms, mantle, natural resource, prevailing wind, regions, relief, river system, temperate zone, tropical zone

SKILL POWER: CRITICAL THINKING

UNDERSTANDING CAUSE AND EFFECT

For every event, there is a cause. The resulting action is the effect. Fill in the blanks below to show cause and effect.

CAUSE		EFFECT
1. Movement	→	_____ _____
2. Heat from earth's core	→	_____
3. Waterways	→	_____
4. Earth's tilted axis	→	_____
5. _____ _____ _____	→	Climate

Name _____ Date _____ Class _____

LANDFORMS PROFILE

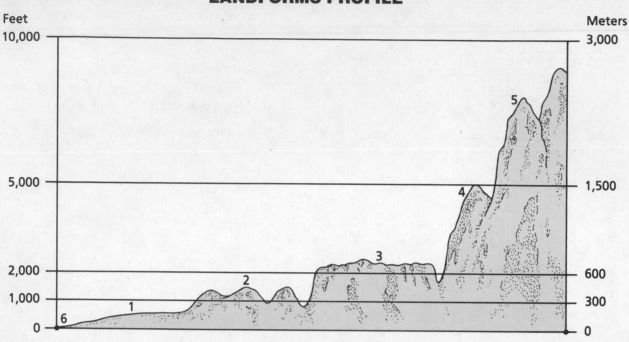

Throughout time, landforms have affected history in a variety of ways. Use the diagram above and your text to answer the following questions.

A. Identify the landforms indicated by the numbers on the diagram:

1. _____

2. _____

3. _____

4. _____

B. Could the place numbered 5 be the highest peak in the Himalayas? _____ Why or why not?

_____

Could number 4 be called Mt. Mitchell? _____ Why or why not? _____

_____

What name do geographers give the place at 0 feet that is numbered 6 on the diagram? _____

_____

C. _____ rise at least 2,000 feet, or 600 meters, above sea level.

_____ have elevations that range from 300 feet, or 90 meters, to more than 3,000 feet, or 900 meters.

Prehistoric People

FOCUS ON IDEAS

Fill in each blank to form a summary of Chapter 2 by choosing the proper term from the words listed below.

\artists	fire	language	\specialization
\chief	\food suppliers	\nature	\toolmakers
\clothing	\government	\Neanderthals	\tools
\domesticate	\herders	\prehistoric	\trade
\farming	\home territory	\priest	\villages

The first _____ age is called the Paleolithic Age. People lived in small bands of about 20 members. Each of these bands gathered food and hunted within an area known as its _____ _____. Paleolithic people learned to make _____. The discovery of how to make _____ enabled them to cook their food. _____ was devised from animal skins held together by long strips of animal hide. The simple sounds of early people developed into _____ as people began to need to cooperate.

Homo sapiens, or "man who thinks," is the name given to two groups of prehistoric people. _____ were good hunters, good builders, and were probably the first people to bury their dead. The second group, Cro-Magnons, were skillful _____, which enabled them to hunt and farm more easily, and become _____ and trading people who met with other groups to exchange information.

Around 8000 B.C., people started to get most of their food from ___farmi___. As they learned to _____, or tame animals, they became _____. Soon people were able to settle in one place and build villages. Due to the Neolithic Revolution, increased _____ _____ led to an increase in population. The beginning of occupations, or _____, helped people to work at new jobs, and they became potters, metalworkers, and weavers. _____ began as finished goods were exchanged for food items. Gradually, new ideas about _____ and religion developed. Power was held by a single _____, who was a _____ as well as a ruler. Neolithic people created gods and goddesses to represent the forces of _____ that they saw around them.

USING VOCABULARY

Unscramble the letters in the first column to spell out the term being described in the second column. Then write the unscrambled word in the spaces in the third column. Next, write the circled letters from the third column in order from top to bottom in the spaces provided for the word puzzler at the end of the activity. Finally, write a definition for the word puzzler on the line provided.

rtoypeishr	time before humans developed writing	_ _ _ _ _ _ _ _ _ _
nsbad	groups of early people who lived together	Ⓞ _ _ _ _
settmedcioa	to tame animals	_ _ _ _ _ _ _ _ _ _
iplnotuaop	number of people	_ _ _ Ⓞ _ _ _ _ _ _
ehmo tyretrori	a known amount of land space for hunting and living	_ _ _ _ _ _ Ⓞ _ _ _ _ _
igteram	make a way to another place	_ _ _ _ _ _ _
sotp-nda-tlienl	length of wood or stone placed across two upright poles	_ _ _ _ - _ _ _ _ - _ _ _ _ _ _ _
vziiilnotcai	began when people started to live in cities and advanced cultures	_ Ⓞ _ _ _ _ _ _ _ _ _ _
npcoatlisizaie	development of occupations	_ _ _ _ _ _ _ _ _ _ _ _ _ Ⓞ

??Word Puzzler?? _____   _ _ _ _ _

"WHAT IT'S LIKE TO BE A . . ."

A. Identify the occupations shown in the squares by writing the name in the blank provided.

Briefly explain what people do in each occupation shown

1. _____   _____

_____

2. _____   _____

_____

BEING A NEOLITHIC CHIEF

A.   *Imagine that you must take over the responsibilities of a chief in a Neolithic village. On the lines below, list separately your government duties and your religious duties.*

<u>Government Duties</u>	<u>Religious Duties</u>
1. _____	1. _____
2. _____	2. _____
3. _____	3. _____

B.   *Look at your lists and answer the following two questions on the lines provided.*

1. What qualifications do you think Neolithic leaders had to have in order to carry out duties?

_____

_____

_____

_____

_____

_____

2. Do you think the same qualifications apply to modern government leaders? Why or why not?

_____

_____

_____

_____

_____

_____

_____

_____

_____

Name _____ Date _____ Class _____

Use the scene of prehistoric life to answer the questions below.

1. What does the woman in the foreground seem to be doing? _____
    _____

2. What do you think these people used to store food? _____

3. Do the pigs look wild or domesticated? _____

4. What does the woman on the right side of the picture appear to be doing? _____
    _____

5. Do these dwellings look permanent? _____

6. For what activities might the fire be used? _____
    _____

7. What time period do you think is represented in this picture, Paleolithic or Neolithic?
    _____

    Why? _____
    _____
    _____

Geography and History

UNDERSTANDING THE FIVE THEMES OF GEOGRAPHY

From geographers, archaeologists, and other scientists, we know that peoples' lifestyles have been influenced by their environments. Imagine that you can create your own community. Use the five themes of geography to guide you in developing your community.

1. **Location: Where is it?**
   Locate your community somewhere on the earth using lines of latitude and longitude. Use directions to tell both absolute and relative location.

   Absolute location: Latitude _____   Longitude _____

   Relative location: Located by _____

   _____

2. **Place: What is it like?**
   Physical Characteristics:
   Climate, landforms, and waterways _____

   Animal life and plants available _____

   Human Characteristics: What is the language? Is it spoken or written? _____

3. **Human/Environmental Interaction:**

		Environmental Interaction		
	What the People Do	Using?	Adapting?	Changing?
Food Supply				
Clothing				
Shelter				

4. **Movement: How is your community linked with other people?**

   Trade _____

   Communication _____

   Transportation _____

5. **Region: What word or phrase could be used to generalize about your community's citizens?**

   _____

Name _____ Date _____ Class _____

UNIT 1 — AROUND THE WORLD

PREHISTORIC PEOPLES OF THE SAHARA

THE SAHARA

The world's largest desert—the Sahara—today looks nothing like it did in prehistoric times. Fill in the lines below to show a comparison of what we know today to what we think it looked like in the past. Use textbook pages 48–49 to help you complete the page.

	Prehistoric Times	**Today**
Vegetation		
Waterways		
Animals		
Human Occupation		

What evidence have archaeologists found in the Sahara to prove that during the prehistoric era the land supported a more livable environment? _____

_____

Imagine that you are an inhabitant of prehistoric Sahara. Below, draw a sketch of one animal or reptile that you may have seen on the grasslands.

Mesopotamia

FOCUS ON IDEAS

Fill in each blank to form a summary of Chapter 3 by choosing the proper term from the words listed below.

barley	Euphrates	monarchy	Sargon I
bricks	god	palace	small villages
businesses	Hammurabi	pipes	Sumerians
canals	kings	priests	surplus
city-states	law code	property	temple
Egyptians	Mesopotamia	rice	Tigris
empire		write	

Civilization began in _____, an area of the Middle East located between the

_____ and _____ rivers. There, people known as _____

learned to control the floodwaters of the rivers. They used _____ to bring the water to

their crops. The main building materials were sunbaked _____ made from mud and

reeds.

This early civilization consisted of a group of _____. Life in each of these com-

munities centered on the _____. This building was believed to be the home of the city's

chief _____. The temple schools prepared students for work in business and govern-

ment by teaching them how to _____. Only males went to school. Women, however,

did have the right to buy and sell _____ and to run businesses.

Powerful _____ ran the schools and managed the land in the name of the gods.

At one time, they were also political leaders. Later, military leaders replaced them as permanent

_____.

Around 2300 B.C., _____, a ruler from northern Mesopotamia, conquered all of

the region. He created the world's first _____. Later, _____, king of

Babylon, controlled Mesopotamia. He united the people by setting up a single _____

_____. By trading their _____, or extra, products, the Babylonians creat-

ed an important trade center.

USING VOCABULARY

Chapter 3

A. *Complete the puzzle using the clues given below.*

1. _ C _ _ _ _   1. a writer
2. _ _ _ _ I _ _ _ _   2. Sumerian writing
3. _ _ _ _ _ _ _ T _   3. "mountain of god"
4. _ _ _ _ _ _ _ _ _ Y   4. passed down from parent to child
5. _ _ _ _ _ _ _ _ - _ _ _ _ _ 5. Sumerian rulers
6. _ _ _ _ _ S   6. raised areas of soil
7. _ _ _ T _ _ _   7. way of life
8. _ _ _ _ A _ _ _ _   8. moving from one place to another
9. _ _ T _ _ _ _ _   9. skilled workers
10. _ E _ _ _   10. period of power

B. *In the space below, draw your impression of a Sumerian city-state.*

Name _____ Date _____ Class _____

CUNEIFORM MESSAGE

Imagine that you are a Sumerian teenager writing a message to a friend. On the lines below, tell about your daily life at school or at home.

(Answers may vary.)

Thank you for your letter. I am now attending school. Classes

are held in rooms off the temple courtyards. I am learning how

to write and hope someday to be a scribe in my father's busi-

ness. He is a merchant. Hope to see you during the holidays.

Write to me about your plans for the future.

_____

_____

_____

SKILL POWER: CRITICAL THINKING

DISTINGUISHING FACT FROM OPINION

In preparing a write-up for a social studies report, a student has written the following paragraph about the people of early Sumer. Help the student ensure that only factual information is given. On the line following each sentence, write an "F" if the statement is a fact and an "O" if it is an opinion. For the opinion sentences, underline the word or words that tell you the sentence is an opinion.

People of Early Sumer

Southern Mesopotamia was settled by short, stocky, black-haired people. _____ I think that they had to learn to work together as they used an excellent and complex system of irrigation canals for farming. _____ Their houses were built from sun-baked bricks. _____ Sumerians were probably the first city-builders of the world. _____ A temple called a ziggurat was at the center of their city. _____ It usually stored the goods of farmers, artisans, and traders. _____ Boys of the rich went to school there since they were the only people who could afford it. _____ Other people might have had their children helping in their trade or farming. _____ Women could buy and sell property, among other rights that they had. _____ Sumerians were ruled by priest-kings who might have been very kind. _____

Name _____ Date _____ Class _____

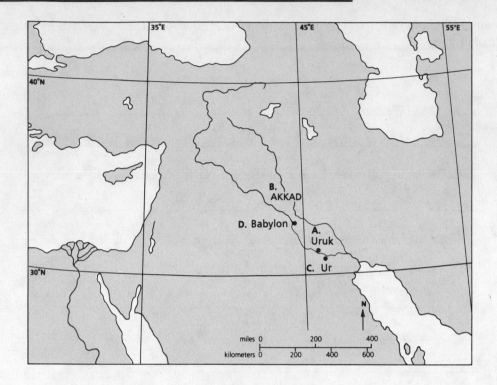

On the map above, label the following: Mediterranean Sea, Black Sea, Red Sea, Caspian Sea, Nile River, Tigris River, Euphrates River, Persian Gulf, Mesopotamia. Then, note that several of the city-states and regions have been labeled with letters. Match these places with the descriptions given below.

1. _____ one of the great city-states of Sumer

2. _____ city-state where Gilgamesh was priest-king

3. _____ area ruled by Sargon I

4. _____ city-state ruled by Hammurabi

Egypt

FOCUS ON IDEAS

Fill in each blank to form a summary of Chapter 4 by choosing the proper term from the words listed below.

Amon-Re	decline	Middle Kingdom	religion
Amenhotep IV	delta	New Kingdom	rulers
Assyrian	floods	Nile River	Tigris River
basins	Hyksos	Old Kingdom	trade
Catal Hüyük	improve	palaces	tombs
	life after death	pharaohs	war

The Egyptians built a civilization in the _____ _____ valley that lasted for more than 2,000 years. For growing crops they depended on the rich soil left by the river's yearly floods. To hold water during the dry season, the Egyptians dug bowl-shaped holes called _____. Most Egyptians lived where the Nile River branches into a fan-shaped area called a(n) _____.

A period known as the _____ _____ began when Narmer united the regions of Upper Egypt and Lower Egypt into one nation. The kings of Egypt became known as _____. They were viewed by the Egyptians as _____, priests, and gods. Egyptian religion stressed the importance of _____ _____ _____. Pyramids were built as _____ for the early Egyptian kings.

The _____ _____ began around 1950 B.C. and lasted until the _____ invaded Egypt in 1786 B.C. After the Egyptians defeated the invaders around 1500 B.C., a period known as the _____ _____ began. During this time, most Egyptian rulers were interested mainly in _____, and they established a large empire. Powerful priests used wealth gained from trade to build temples in honor of the god _____. In 1370 B.C., a ruler named _____ opposed the priests and tried to set up a new _____. Toward the end of this period of conflict, Egyptian civilization began to decline.

USING VOCABULARY

Write a complete definition for each vocabulary word listed below. Then, match each vocabulary word with the correct picture on the right by placing the letter of the picture after the proper definition in the blank provided.

Shadoof _____	**A**
Papyrus _____	**B**
Pharaoh _____	**C**
Pyramid _____	**D**
Hieroglyphic _____	**E**
Mummy _____	**F**

WORD CLUES: People and Places

A. *Read the clues given for people and places in the first column. Then, write the answers on the lines provided in the second column.*

1. "gift of the Nile" _____

2. first ruler of a united Egypt _____

3. god of harvest and eternal life _____

4. female pharaoh _____

5. Akhenaton _____

6. popular Egyptian goddess _____

7. desert invaders of Egypt _____

B. *Select three of the answers above and explain how the ancient Egyptians were affected by this person(s) or place.*

1._____

_____

_____

_____

2._____

_____

_____

_____

_____

3._____

_____

_____

_____

_____

Name _____ Date _____ Class _____

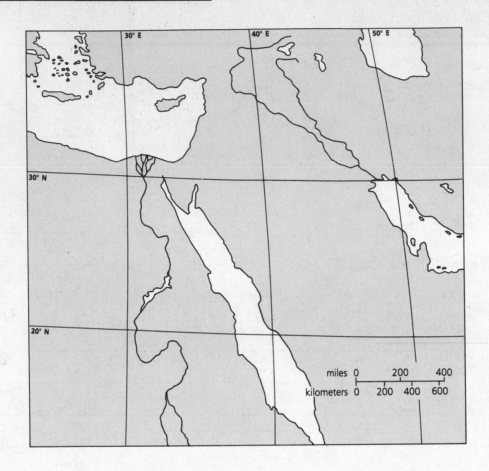

A. On the map above, label the following: Africa, Mediterranean Sea, Red Sea, Nile River, Nile Delta, Lower Egypt, Upper Egypt, Syria, Palestine, Memphis, Thebes.

B. Read the statements below that describe a feature or place labeled on the map. Fill in the blanks with the name of the correct feature or place.

_____

_____   1. kingdom located in the south of Egypt

_____   2. body of water north of Egypt

_____   3. kingdom located in the north of Egypt

_____   4. river flowing north from central Africa

_____   5. Narmer's capital city

_____   6. city known for its god, Amon

_____   7. fan-shaped area of fertile land

_____   8. areas conquered by New Kingdom
                                            pharaohs

_____   9. continent in which Egypt is located

Eastern River Valleys

Chapter
5

FOCUS ON IDEAS

Fill in each blank to form a summary of Chapter 5 by choosing the proper term from the words listed below.

agreement	✓Egypt	✓Mesopotamia	rich
ancestors	farming	mountains	Shang
✓Aryans	✓Harappans	oracle bones	spirits
cities	✓Huang Ho	✓ovens	✓trading
✓cotton	✓Indus River	✓plan	warrior-king
countryside	man-god	poor	Zhou

Civilizations developed in the _____ _____ valley of South Asia and the _____ _____ Valley of China. The people of these civilizations were more isolated than the people of _____ and _____. They also did less _____ and learned to take care of all their needs.

The _____ were the first people to create a civilization in the Indus River valley. Experts believe they may have been the first people to make _____ cloth, to bake bricks in _____, and to build cities according to a definite _____. Little is known about the causes for the decline of this civilization. However, it is known that a group of people known as _____ took over the Indus River valley around 1200 B.C.

According to legend, a(n) _____ named Yü founded the Huang Ho Valley civilization. The first records of this civilization came from a ruling family known as _____. They built the first _____ in the region. However, most of the people lived in the _____.

The Shang worshipped _____ and paid respect to _____. Kings made important decisions by consulting _____ _____. Experts believe the distance between _____ and _____ weakened the Shang civilization. In 1122 B.C., a people known as _____ conquered the kingdom.

Name _____ Date _____ Class _____

Fill in the squares by spelling out the terms given in the clues below.

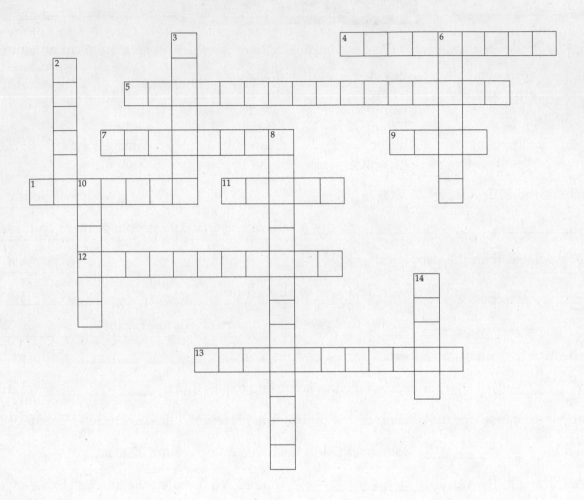

ACROSS

1. a ruling family
4. people from whom one descends
5. city built to a definite plan
7. fortresses
9. uniform network of streets
11. ovens used to make bricks
12. blue stone used for jewelry
13. has the oldest known form of Chinese writing

DOWN

2. a place where a river flows
3. storage for grain
6. supernatural beings
8. able to care for one's own needs
10. people of high rank
14. baked in a kiln

PEOPLE OF THE EASTERN RIVER VALLEYS

The two paragraphs below might have been written by members of ancient eastern river valley civilizations. Paragraph A was written by a noble in Shang China explaining the effect the nobles had on the lives of the peasants. Paragraph B is by a Harappan soldier expressing pride in his city. Read the paragraphs and answer the questions that follow.

A.   "I guide the peasants as they work the fields to provide foods for the country. Most of the soldiers under my command are peasants. We nobles require them to leave their farms and join the army when we need them. I like to wear expensive clothes made of silk. The silk is produced by our peasant workers. Usually, I am not concerned about the peasants. Their lives are very different from ours. Nobles and peasants have little in common."

What does this paragraph tell you about Shang society? _____

_____

_____

How do you think the peasants felt about their role in Shang society? _____

_____

_____

B.   "I stand at guard on the citadel wall. I am proud of Mohenjodaro. It is my greatest wish that the floods do not damage my home this year. In view are the straight streets of our organized city. It is good that we have continued the plan of our ancestors. Our city prospers most of the time. We are known for our attention to a clean, healthy community."

Why is the soldier proud of his city? _____

What clues are given to possible future problems? _____

_____

_____

_____

Name _____ Date _____ Class _____

The sketches below show two artifacts from the eastern river valley civilizations. Study them to answer the questions below.

Shang Bronze Sculpture

Harappan Soapstone Seal

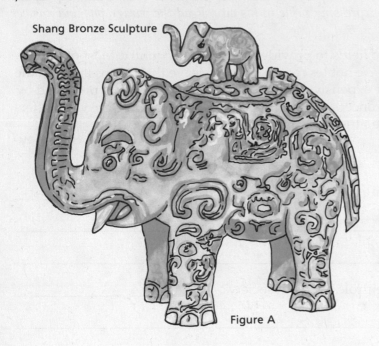

Figure A

Figure B

1. What do these artifacts have in common? _____

2. Which seems to be more real or life-like? _____ Why? _____

   _____

3. Which figure appears to be more imaginative? _____ Why? _____

   _____

4. What use might Figure A have had for its owner? _____

   _____

5. What was Figure B used for? _____

6. Who might have owned and used Figure B? _____

   _____

Geography and History

GEOGRAPHY THEMES IN RIVER VALLEY CIVILIZATIONS

Use textbook maps and other resources to fill in the chart below to compare facts about the location, place, and region of different river valleys. Then use your chart to answer the questions below.

Civilization	Mesopotamia	Egypt	Indus Valley	Huang Ho Valley
Dates				
Latitudinal Location				
Region				
Landform				
Climate				
Ways to Make a Living				

1. Which area probably had the coolest weather? _____ Why do you think

   this is true? _____

   _____

2. List at least 2 things that were common to all of these areas. _____

3. Why did early people settle in these areas? _____

   _____

   _____

4. What determines the direction a river flows? _____

   _____

UNIT 2 AROUND THE WORLD

THE HITTITES

Answer the following questions in complete sentences. Use textbook pages 94–95 to help you complete the page.

1. What evidence has caused archaeologists to believe the Hittites chose to rule conquered people by treaty?

   _____

   _____

2. Why do we believe the Hittites were creative people?

   _____

   _____

3. What was the most effective weapon or invention the Hittites used in conquest?

   _____

SEPARATING FACT FROM OPINION

Read each of the following statements about the Hittites and decide whether it is a fact or an opinion. In the space provided, write "F" for Fact and "O" for Opinion.

1. _____ The Hittites used the anger of the gods to threaten people who broke their laws or treaties.

2. _____ Hittite people were more creative than the Egyptians.

3. _____ Records of Hittite treaties were placed on metal tablets.

4. _____ The sun was the most important symbol in the Hittite religion.

BEING CREATIVE: Design a Hittite Royal Seal

Imagine that you serve in the Hittite Empire as an artist. Design a Royal Seal for a child of the Hittite king in the space below.

The Phoenicians and the Hebrews

Chapter 6

FOCUS ON IDEAS

Fill in each blank to form a summary of Chapter 6 by choosing the proper term from the words listed below.

alphabet	farmers	Judaism	Pacific
Bible	free speech	laws	prophets
Canaan	Israel	Mediterranean	rivers
cedar	Jerusalem	merchants	sabbath
David	jewelry	Moses	sea
dye	Judah	oak	social justice

The Phoenicians lived in the northern part of _____. Their region was famous

for its _____ forests and an expensive purple _____. Because farmland

was limited, many Phoenicians turned to the _____ for a living. They brought the cul-

ture of the Middle East to unexplored areas of the western _____. One of the most

important contributions they passed along to other peoples was the idea of a(n)

_____.

The early Hebrews were traveling _____. According to the _____,

God made an agreement with Abraham that gave Canaan to the Hebrews if they accepted Him alone

as the one true god. After a long stay in Egypt, the Hebrews were led by _____ into the

desert. There, they made another agreement with God and promised to obey certain

_____.

A strong Hebrew kingdom later emerged in Canaan under the rule of _____.

His son, Solomon, built a huge temple in the capital city of _____. The Hebrew king-

dom finally split into the kingdoms of _____ and _____. During this

time, _____ reminded the Hebrews of their duty to God and neighbor. Some of them

taught the idea of _____ _____ for everybody. Although the Hebrew

kingdoms did not last, the Hebrew religion still exists today and is called _____.

USING VOCABULARY

Chapter 6

The alphabetical list contains the letters for spelling the words that complete the statements below. Complete the statements with the proper word, and cross out the letters used to spell the answers. When all of the statements have been completed, all letters in the alphabetical list will have been used.

A A A A A A A A A B B C C C C C C C D D D D

D E E E E E E E E E F G H H H H H I I I I I J J

L L L L L L M M M N N N N N N N O O O O O

O O O O O P R R R R S S S S S S S S S S S S

T T T T T T U U U U U V X X Y Y

1. What is the name of the shellfish that yields a purple dye? _____

2. What term is given to ornamental vases used by Phoenicians for burial? _____

3. What phrase is used to explain the most sacred chamber in a temple? _____

4. What term is given to wandering herders? _____

5. What are the sacred songs found in the Bible called? _____

6. What name is given to the escape of a great number of people from oppression?

   _____

7. What was an agreement between the Hebrew people and Yahweh called? _____

8. What is another name for offspring, the children of parents? _____

9. What term was given to the permanent settlements of Phoenicians as they sailed the Mediter-

   ranean area? _____

10. What word is used to describe an agreement between countries? _____

11. Rolls of parchment on which Hebrews wrote their laws and stories were called

    _____.

12. What was the leader of a Hebrew tribe called? _____

13. What is the phrase that describes the Hebrew belief of how each individual should be treated

    fairly? _____

14. The laws of Moses were written in five books called the _____.

15. Like other Middle Eastern countries the Hebrews had a day of rest to pray and discuss religion.

    It is called the _____.

COMMUNICATIONS ACROSS TIME

VOL. I
NO. 3

PHOENICIAN TIMES

EVENING
EDITION

NEW WRITING SYSTEM IN PHOENICIA

GROWTH OF TRADE

CARTHAGE FOUNDED

Carthage

Mediterranean Sea

AFRICA

SKILL POWER: CRITICAL THINKING

MAKING COMPARISONS

Complete the chart below comparing Phoenician and Hebrew ways of living. Use textbook pages 101–114 for help.

Daily Needs	Phoenicians	Hebrews
Food	shopped/traded wherever they were	
Shelter		
Clothing		
Government		12 tribes; used social justice

WORKING WITH MAPS

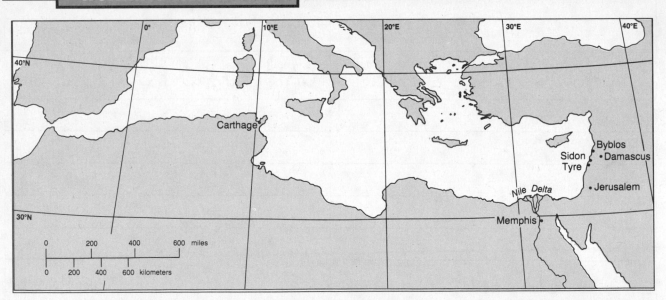

On the map above, label the following: Mediterranean Sea, Israel, Phoenicia, Egypt. Study the map and answer the questions that follow.

1. What is the distance from Carthage to Sidon? _____

2. If travelers from Tyre make an overland journey to Memphis, in which two directions do they

    travel? _____

3. What is the distance from Damascus to Jerusalem? _____

4. What direction is Jerusalem from Memphis? _____

MILITARY EMPIRES

Chapter 7

FOCUS ON IDEAS

Fill in each blank to form a summary of Chapter 7 by choosing the proper term from the words listed below.

Ashurbanipal	cruelty	Egyptian Empire	Persepolis
army	Cyrus	planets	Persian Empire
astronomers	eastern Europe	merchants	provinces
Babylon	fairness	navy	roads
canals	Hittites	Nebuchadrezzar	cities
central Asia	iron	Nineveh	Zoroaster

The Assyrians developed a well-organized _____ and conquered a large area of the

Middle East. They were especially skilled in attacking _____ and were feared because

of their _____. Assyrian strength was due partly to the use of weapons made of

_____. The Assyrians learned the skill of making such weapons from the Hittites.

Assyrian kings divided the empire into _____. These areas were linked by a system

of _____. In time, the empire started to fall apart. In 612 B.C., the Chaldeans captured

_____, the Assyrian capital.

The Chaldean king, _____, built a new capital at _____ that became

the center of a great civilization. Chaldean _____ studied the heavens and made maps

that plotted the positions of the _____. Chaldean territory later became a part of the

_____ _____.

The Persians came from _____ _____ and settled on a high plain be-

tween the Persian Gulf and the Caspian Sea. Under King _____, they began to develop

a large empire. Persian rulers were known for their _____ toward conquered peoples.

During this time, a religious leader named _____ taught a new religion that stressed

the struggle between good and evil.

USING VOCABULARY

Find and circle in the box of letters below the eight terms listed in the first column. Some of the words appear horizontally, some vertically, and others diagonally. After you have found the terms, describe or identify them on the line provided in the second column.

```
C S H S M E L T I N G L M
A H A D U R I E M U V Y A
R R R E K M T E M L D O R
A H A I S W T E O M T B D
V A F M M D E Z R J P R U
A L Y D A A R V T D N X K
N D I U O I N P A M U T I
S E C P B I C D L X O K C
P R O V I N C E S U Z A L
D A S T R O N O M E R S A
```

Term	Description
litter	_____
Marduk	_____
Immortals	_____
smelting	_____
astronomers	_____
provinces	_____
caravans	_____
Aramaic	_____

EMPIRES OF THE MIDDLE EAST

Complete the following chart to show a comparison of the military empires of the Middle East from 2300 B.C. to 479 B.C. Use the phrases listed below the chart for your answers.

	Reasons for Success	Treatment of Their Subjects	Method of Control	Contributions
Assyrians	• well-organized powerful army • _____	• _____ • heavy taxes	• divided empire into provinces • _____	• first world library
Chaldeans	• _____ • used knowledge to gain wealth	• used them as slaves • demanded worship of their gods	• tribute paid to them yearly • _____	• _____ • "hanging gardens"
Persians	• _____ • desire to rule other peoples	• allowed subjects to keep their own language, religion, and laws • _____	• _____ • had "King's Eyes and Ears" to inspect the outlying areas	• _____ • Royal Road system • use of coins as money

A. divided into 20 provinces

B. strong, huge army

C. Zoroaster taught belief in two gods

D. use of iron weapons

E. huge brick walls encircled their capital

F. believed in fairness

G. killed the defeated

H. center of science

I. road system

J. built a very large capital

WORKING WITH MAPS

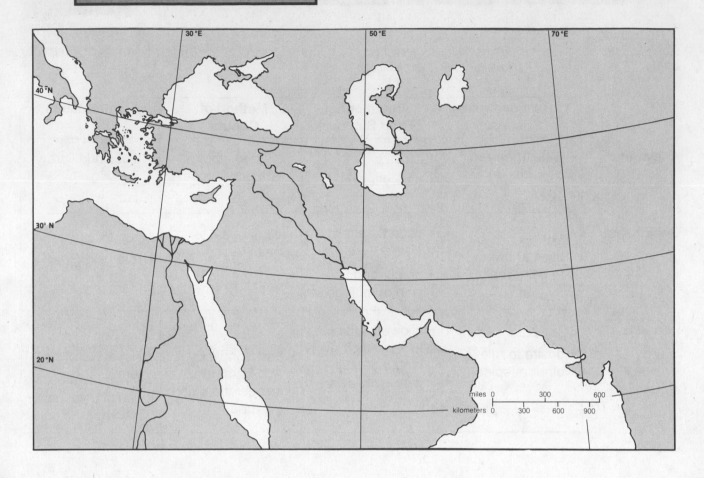

A. *On the map above, label the following: Mediterranean Sea, Caspian Sea, Red Sea, Black Sea, Persian Gulf, Tigris River, Euphrates River. Also label: Egypt, Persia, Chaldea, Israel, Judah, Phoenicia, Assyria, Lydia, Asia Minor. Draw in the Royal Road of the Persian Empire.*

B. *Fill in the blanks below with the names of the cities being described in the statements. Label the cities on the map. Use dots to show their locations.*

_____ 1. Assyrian capital taken by the Chaldeans

_____ 2. Chaldean capital known as the world's richest city

_____ 3. Persian city famous for its palace-fortress-treasury

_____ 4. city of Asia Minor located on the Royal Road

_____ 5. Persian city located farthest east on the Royal Road

AFRICA AND THE AMERICAS

FOCUS ON IDEAS

Fill in each blank to form a summary of Chapter 8 by choosing the proper term from the words listed below.

Aksum	iron-smelting	Olmecs	South America
brick-making	language	palace	Swahili
bronze	maize	pilgrimage	Tenochtitlán
Central America	mathematicians	salt	terraces
deserts	Meroë	savannahs	trading
East	nomads	slag	university

On the East African grassy plains, or _____, the ancient kingdom of Kush was built

by _____, or wandering herders. Kushites learned from the Egyptians the worship of

Amon-Re and the skill of working copper and _____; and from the Assyrians, the secret

of _____. Kush began as a great trading country but declined, being replaced by

_____. Aksum was successful at trade and learned how to farm on , _____or

raised levels of land.

In West Africa, Ghana, Mali, and Songhai rose to power as _____ kingdoms. Their

strengths lay in the trade of gold and _____ and the knowledge of iron-smelting. One

king of Mali became famous as he made a _____ to Arabia and gave gold to poor peo-

ple. Mansa Musa I also built a _____ at Timbuktu.

Zimbabwe and Kilwa, two East African countries, became great trading kingdoms and dealt in gold,

copper, and ivory with countries of the _____. In Kilwa, a culture called _____

developed as a blend of civilizations.

Across the globe, in the Americas, two ancient trading civilizations, the _____ and

Mayas, flourished. They developed planned cities and a calendar. The Mayas proved themselves to

be great astronomers and _____. Two other controllers of _____

_____ and _____ _____ were the warlike nations of the Aztecs

and the Incas. A capital built at _____ gave the Aztecs control over Mesoamerica. The

Incas built a strong empire through a road system and a common religion and _____.

USING VOCABULARY

The scrambled words at the beginning of each sentence contain the letters for the two terms needed. Cross off, in order, the letters necessary for the first definition and the term for the second definition will be left. The first one has been completed as an example.

1.   TE~~S~~R~~A~~V~~A~~R~~N~~A~~N~~C~~A~~E~~H~~S

   Remove a grassy plain, _____savannah_____, and leave _____terraces_____, raised levels of land.

2.   NPIOLGMARIDMAIGCE

   Remove wandering cattle herders, _____, and leave _____, a religious journey.

3.   CAAQUUSEDEUWCATYSS

   Removed paved roads, _____, and leave _____, water channels.

4.   SRIELFEUNGTBAERETESR

   Remove a trading technique, _____ _____, and leave

   _____, people who flee for safety.

5.   QZUIEPRUOS

   Remove counting devices, _____, and leave _____, a Mayan mathematics idea.

6.   MSAILZAEG

   Remove shiny, black waste, _____, and leave _____, corn.

"WHAT WAS IT LIKE TO BE A . . ."

A. *Study the four drawings. Identify possible occupations of early African and American civilizations by writing the name of each in the blank provided.*

Africa	America
1._____	3._____
2._____	4._____

B. *Briefly explain what the people might have done in each of the occupations shown above.*

1._____

_____

2._____

_____

3._____

_____

4._____

_____

Name _____ Date _____ Class _____

The civilizations of Mesoamerica worshipped many gods and goddesses. The picture below shows the Mayan Goddess of Corn from the Dresden Codex, one of the few Mayan works still existing. Study the picture to help you answer the questions below. You may need to use your textbook for assistance.

1. What is the figure holding in her hand? _____

2. Why would the Mayas include this goddess in their religion? _____

   _____

3. Why do you think the goddess might look angry? _____

   _____

4. What religious ceremony do we know the Mayas engaged in? _____

   _____

   _____

5. The peoples of Mesoamerica believed in gods and goddesses that represented natural things.

   You looked at the Goddess of Corn above. What are some other gods that the Mesoamericans

   might have worshipped? _____

   _____

Geography and History

UNIT 3

THE SPREAD OF TECHNOLOGY

Geographers study movement—how people and places are linked together. Some factual highlights about the Phoenicians are given below. Study these highlights to complete the paragraphs at the bottom of the page.

HIGHLIGHT 1: Phoenicians settled on a narrow strip of land along the eastern Mediterranean Sea, which had a little fertile soil but not enough to feed the people. Forested mountains were nearby.

HIGHLIGHT 2: To make a living, Phoenicians looked to the sea. Lumber from the mountains was used to build strong, fast ships.

HIGHLIGHT 3: Phoenicians traveled from place to place, trading cedar logs, cloth, and glass items for gold and other metals.

HIGHLIGHT 4: Phoenician sailors became confident as they plotted their courses by the sun and stars. Trading posts eventually became colonies of Phoenicia.

HIGHLIGHT 5: In order to trade, Phoenicians had to communicate with people who spoke a variety of languages. To keep track of trading records, they changed picture writing to a simpler method of writing.

HIGHLIGHT 6: Wherever the Phoenicians traveled, they shared ideas from one group to another increasing knowledge and improving life.

1. Explain how the phoenicians used transportation to make a living. _____

   _____

   _____

2. Describe how Phoenicians adapted their forms of communication as their trade developed.

   _____

   _____

3. After you compare Highlights 1 and 6, explain the statement, "Geography greatly affected the

   Phoenicians and eventually affected all of Europe." _____

   _____

   _____

UNIT 3 — AROUND THE WORLD

THE ZHOU

In today's world, you see or hear advertising slogans for products and services everywhere you go. Imagine that similar slogans existed during the Zhou dynasty. Use textbook pages 144–145 to help you complete the page.

A Job Advertisement

> Wanted: Military planner, self-starter, highly motivated.
> Positive attitude. Excellent job security.

This ad relates to the historical fact that the Zhou dynasty was involved in constant warfare.

A. *For the advertisements below, write the historical facts to which they refer.*

Advertisement	Historical Fact
1. Secret hideaway—most civilized spot in the world. Sit back, relax, and listen to music drifting into your suite.	_____ _____ _____
2. Attend our seminar, "Update on Use of the Iron Plow and Other Complex Farming Methods" at the Community Center. This is a must for all farmers.	_____ _____ _____

B. *For the historical facts given below, write your own advertising slogan.*

1. _____ _____	The Zhou family life had close and strong traditions.
2. _____ _____	One of the Zhou's cultural accomplishments was the creation of ornate metal objects.

Name _____ Date _____ Class _____

 # Beginnings

FOCUS ON IDEAS

Fill in the blanks to form a summary of Chapter 9. You will find some of the proper terms listed below. For other words, you may need to use your textbook.

civil wars	fortress-palaces	laws	park
Crete	gymnasiums	Mother Earth	seafaring
Dark Age	Hellenes	navigation	Troy
farmers	Knossos	*Odyssey*	walls

Minoan civilization developed on the island of _____. At first, Minoans were

_____. Later, they became the world's first important _____ civilization.

Minoan cities were different from those of other ancient civilizations. At the center of each city was

a _____ rather than a temple. Minoan cities did not have _____ around

them. Instead people relied on their _____ for protection. One of the largest Minoan

cities was _____.

Minoans worshipped many gods and goddesses. They especially honored the goddess

_____ _____. Minoan priest-kings made _____ and ex-

plained the gods' will by looking for signs from the sky at the top of _____

_____.

About 1400 B.C., the _____ took control of the Aegean area. They learned many

things from Minoans, especially the skills of shipbuilding and _____. They formed

_____ _____ to raid nearby lands. Their attack on the city of

_____ is told in an epic poem called the *Iliad*.

Weakened by years of _____ _____, Mycenaeans were defeated by the

_____. As a result, the Aegean region entered a _____. In isolation from

the rest of the Middle East, a new civilization began. Its people formed small independent communi-

ties and started calling themselves _____.

USING VOCABULARY

Write a complete definition for each vocabulary word listed below. Then, match each vocabulary word with the correct picture on the right by placing the letter of the picture after the proper definition in the blank provided. Where none is provided, draw a sketch of the vocabulary word.

labyrinth _____

_____

_____ ___

A

bull leaping _____

_____

_____ ___

B

megaron _____

_____

_____ ___

C

frescoes _____

_____

_____ ___

D

shrine _____

_____

_____ ___

E

prow _____

_____

_____ ___

F

SPORTS PAST, PRESENT, AND FUTURE

The Minoans enjoyed such sports as boxing and bull leaping. In ancient times, sporting events were largely religious ceremonies performed in honor of the gods. Today, they are mainly a form of exercise or entertainment. What will sporting events of the future be like? In this activity, you will have the chance to design a sporting event as it might be performed 100 years from now.

A. *Select a particular sport of today. On the lines below, describe what possible changes might occur in the sport during the next 100 years. You might wish to write about the goal of the activity, the equipment used, step-by-step plays, and the rewards given to winners.*

_____

_____

_____

_____

_____

_____

_____

_____

_____

B. *In the space below, draw a picture or make a diagram that shows how the future sport described above will be played.*

WORKING WITH MAPS

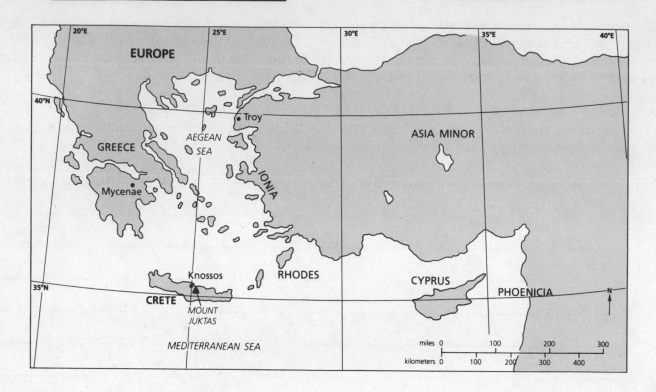

Examine the map and use the scale and directional arrow to answer the questions that follow.

1. In what direction is Crete from Cyprus? _____

2. How far is Knossos from Mycenae? _____

3. How far is Troy from the island of Rhodes? _____

4. In what direction is Iona from Greece? _____

5. In what direction is Troy from Knossos? _____

The City-States

FOCUS ON IDEAS

Fill in the blanks to form a summary of Chapter 10. You will find some of the proper terms listed below. For other words, you may need to use your textbook.

citizens	elections	music	political power
Cleisthenes	government	Pericles	public office
community	Marathon	Persians	truce
democratic	military power	philosophy	war

Around 700 B.C., the _____ became the geographical and political center of Greek life. The _____ in each city-state had certain rights. They could vote, own property, hold _____ _____, and speak for themselves in court. In return, they were expected to take part in _____ and to defend the city-state in time of war.

The two greatest city-states were Sparta and Athens. By 500 B.C., Sparta had become the greatest _____ _____ in Greece. Its aristocrats spent most of their time and energy training for _____. Between 750 and 507 B.C., Athens went through a long series of political _____ that gave more rights to the common people. A noble named _____ put into effect the world's first generally _____ constitution in 507 B.C.

After the defeat of the _____, Athens became the leading city-state of Greece. The main leader of Athens at this time was a general named _____. Under his leadership, art, literature, and _____ advanced greatly.

Sparta defeated Athens in the _____ _____. This struggle weakened the Greek city-states. They soon lost their sense of _____ and were conquered in 338 B.C. by _____ of Macedonia.

USING VOCABULARY   **Chapter 10**

After each clue in Column A, write the answer that fits the spaces in column B.

A	**B**

City-state   p _ _ _ _

Greek marketplace   a _ _ _ _

Spartan merchants and artisans   p _ _ _ _ _ _ _

Fortified hill   a _ _ _ _ _ _ _ _

Spartan slave   h _ _ _ _

Athenian warships   t _ _ _ _ _ _

Greek judge   m _ _ _ _ _ _ _ _

A noble   a _ _ _ _ _ _ _ _

Favoring the equality of all people d _ _ _ _ _ _ _ _

Government where a few people have   o _ _ _ _ _ _ _ _
ruling power

Hired soldier   m _ _ _ _ _ _ _ _ _ _

Set principles and rules for governing c _ _ _ _ _ _ _ _ _ _ _ _
a community

Protective group of Greek city-states   d _ _ _ _ _ _ _ _   _ _ _ _ _ _

Name _____ Date _____ Class _____

RECOGNIZING BIAS

In surfing the Internet, you have found an article which may help you prepare a social studies project on the decline of the Greek city-states. Examine all statements carefully to ensure that you are reporting accurately. Look for any bias the writer may hold. Underline statements that express opinion or emotion. Identify the facts by filling in the blanks.

DECLINE OF THE GREEK CITY-STATES

Powerful Athens was resented by the other Greek city-states. They should have been aware that their attack on one of Sparta's allies would create extreme hostility. The Peloponnesian War, which lasted almost 30 years, was very costly, but a greater loss was felt in the people's attitude. They lost their sense of community. Upper and lower classes clashed. Sparta's harsh rule angered other Greeks until Thebes led other city-states in the overthrow of Sparta. Thebes might have been more successful if their rule had given more freedom to other city-states. In 338 B.C., Philip II of Macedonia conquered a weakened and disunited Greece.

Decline of the Greek city-states was caused by:

1. Who? _____

2. What? _____

3. Where? _____

4. When? _____

KEEPING TRACK OF TIME AND EVENTS

Complete the time chart by placing the letters that represent historical events in Sparta and Athens in the spaces provided beside the dates.

	ATHENS		SPARTA
A. Solon develops a constitution for Athens		800 B.C.	
B. Philip II of Macedonia conquers the Greek city-states		750 B.C.	
		700 B.C.	
C. Sparta defeats Athens in the Peloponnesian War		600 B.C.	
D. Spartan helots and perioeci outnumber aristocrats		594 B.C.	
		560 B.C.	
E. End of the Persian Wars		545 B.C.	
F. Spartan aristocrats overthrow the king		500 B.C.	
G. Athenian nobles and business people take over the government		480 B.C.	
		479 B.C.	
		434 B.C.	
H. Persians conquer Greek city-states in Asia Minor		404 B.C.	
I. King Xerxes defeats Spartans at Thermopylae		371 B.C.	
		338 B.C.	
J. City-state of Thebes defeats Sparta		300 B.C.	

WORKING WITH MAPS

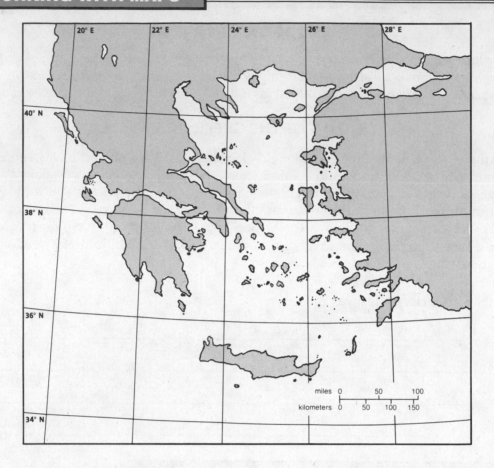

A. On the map above, label: *Mediterranean Sea, Black Sea, Ionian Sea, Aegean Sea, Asia Minor, Macedonia, Persian Empire. Draw in the areas that were part of the Athenian Empire (c. 450 B.C.).*

B. *Fill in the blanks below with the name of the places described in the following statements. Label the places on the map. Use dots to show the locations of cities.*

_____ 1. peninsula of southern Greece

_____ 2. location of the first Greek victory over the Persians

_____ 3. small island to which Athenians fled during Persian attack

_____ 4. location where Persian army was helped by a Greek traitor

_____ 5. two of the greatest Greek city-states

_____ 6. headquarters of the Delian League

Cultural Contributions

FOCUS ON IDEAS

Fill in the blanks to form a summary of Chapter 11. You will find some of the proper terms listed below. For other words, you may need to use your textbook.

Dark Age	Golden Age	Olympic Games	Socratic method
doctors	hypothesis	philosophers	The Academy
Euclid	individual	scientific method	*The Republic*
festivals	laws	Socrates	western

The Greeks were the first people to believe in the freedom and the worth of the

_____. They tried to imitate the _____ by developing their abilities to the

fullest. The result of their efforts was the _____ _____ of Greek culture.

The Greeks celebrated many different kinds of religious _____. Out of them came

important contributions to _____ culture. The _____ _____,

which were held every four years in honor of the god _____, became the most impor-

tant sporting event in Greece. The _____ grew out of celebrations given in honor of the

god Dionysus.

A Greek thinker named _____ placed very great importance on a method of ques-

tioning that helped people arrive at conclusions. Another thinker named _____ set

down his ideas about an ideal state in a book called _____ _____ . Aris-

totle contributed to the advancement of science by creating a system of _____.

Greek scientists believed that the world is governed by natural _____ that

humans can discover and understand. The first Greek scientist, Thales of Miletus, worked out the

first two steps of the _____ _____. Hippocrates contributed to the field

of _____. He drew up a list of rules for _____ known as the Hippocratic

Oath.

USING VOCABULARY

Chapter 11

Under each mystery word, one or more words is missing from the definition. The missing words are clues to the mystery words. Fill in the missing words. Then, in the spaces, spell the mystery words.

— — — — — — —
— — — — — —

a guide for, or _____ of government; *The Republic* explained kinds of governments and how to avoid errors in _____

— — — — — —

humorous Greek drama; the opposite of _____

— — — — — — — — —

study of the laws of nature and the love of _____

— — — — — — — —

conclusion reached by the structure of three _____ statements; deduction

— — — — — — — —

the ability _____ had to predict statements of the future; knowledge desired by Greek people for guidance

— — — — —

the science of _____, or thinking things through

— — — — — — — —

ability to learn and _____; of great importance to Greek scholars

— — — — — — — —

second step of the _____ method; a possible _____ developed after gathering information

— — — — — — — —

in drama, a talk in which personal thoughts and feelings are expressed to an _____

Activity Book

DIALOGUE AND REPORTING

A. *Pretend that you are a student living in Athens during the fourth century* B.C. *On the lines provided, write about an imaginary discussion you might have had with a noted philosopher, such as Socrates, Plato, or Aristotle. Mention the teaching method of the philosopher as well as his ideas.*

_____

_____

_____

_____

_____

_____

_____

_____

_____

_____

B. *Pretend that you are a news reporter covering the trial of Socrates. On the lines below, write an imaginary account of the trial and its outcome. Include the charges made against Socrates as well as the philosopher's defense of his teachings.*

_____

_____

_____

_____

_____

_____

_____

_____

_____

_____

_____

WORKING WITH DIAGRAMS

Greek plays were performed at community festivals. Performances began at sunrise and went on all day. The plays were held in amphitheaters, built into the natural slope of the hillside. Judges, drawn by lottery, awarded prizes to the best writers and actors. The circular orchestra was the stage on which the chorus marched or danced. A permanent backdrop, representing a temple or palace, provided the scenery. No more than three actors appeared at one time. They stood in an area directly in front of the scenery. Spectators viewed the play from the wooden or stone steps.

Use the description above to answer the following questions and label the diagram:

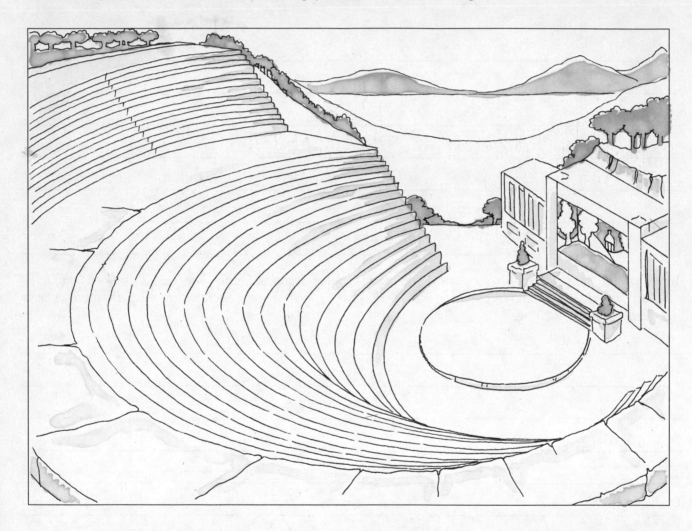

1. Where did the audience sit? _____

2. Where did the chorus members perform? _____

3. Where was the scenery in a Greek play? _____

4. Where did the actors stand? _____

The Hellenistic Period

FOCUS ON IDEAS

Fill in the blanks to form a summary of Chapter 12. You will find some of the proper terms listed below. For other words, you may need to use your textbook.

army	five	Indus	Romans
Classical	free housing	library	three
disagreements	Greeks	navy	Tigris
equal treatment	Hellenistic	Nile	unity

Philip II, king of _____, wanted to unify the Greek city-states under his rule. He developed a strong _____ and caused _____ among Greek leaders. In these ways, he was able to conquer Greece in 338 B.C.

Philip's son Alexander was a great _____ whose conquests stretched from the _____ to the _____ rivers. Alexander tried to bring _____ and justice to his empire. He borrowed many customs from such people as the _____. Alexander also encouraged _____ and Macedonians to settle in new cities scattered all over the empire. These groups, however, objected to _____ _____ for other people. As a result, Alexander's goal was not realized.

The period of Alexander's empire is known as the _____ Age. During this time, trade increased and Greek _____ spread to new areas. The greatest center of trade and learning was _____ in Egypt. It was especially known for its famous _____ staffed by philosophers and scientists.

After Alexander's death, _____ of his generals divided most of the empire among themselves. The Greek city-states eventually regained their freedom. However, they were too weak to resist the _____, who conquered them in 146 B.C.

USING VOCABULARY

Complete the puzzle using the clues given below.

1. _ _ _ _ A _ _

2. _ _ L _ _ _ _ _ _ _

3. _ _ E _ _ _ _ _ _

4. _ _ _ _ _ X

5. _ A _ _ _ _ _ _

6. _ _ _ _ N _ _ _

7. _ _ _ _ _ _ _ _ D

8. _ _ _ _ _ R _

9. _ _ _ _ _ _ I _ _

10. _ _ A _ _ _

Clues

A. 1. a person held by an enemy until certain promises are kept

2. "like the Hellenes"

3. barrier that breaks the force of waves

4. a special infantry formation developed by Philip of Macedonia

5. what the Greeks call Persians

6. partnerships

7. left one place to settle in another

8. subject of Euclid's book

9. places where goods are made

10. a public speaker

B. Write one sentence to describe the importance of the theme word (Alexandria) to the Hellenistic

culture. _____

_____

CORRECT THE STATEMENT

All of the statements below have incorrect information. Underline the mistake in each statement, and write the correction in the space provided.

1. Macedonian kings were of Persian descent.   _____

2. At the same time that Philip came to respect Greek culture, he
    learned to accept the weaknesses of the Greek form of govern-   _____
    ment.

3. Demosthenes encouraged the Greeks to support the Macedo-   _____
    nians.

4. Alexander was a student of Plato.   _____

5. Alexander conquered the Persians and then marched as far east   _____
    as China.

6. The Greeks and Macedonians accepted Alexander's claim that   _____
    he was a god.

7. The most successful new city of Alexander's empire was   _____
    Alexandria, India.

8. A tall fortress stood above the harbor of Alexandria.   _____

9. After Alexander's death, the empire was divided among three   _____
    of the ruler's sons.

10. The cities of Alexander's empire were mainly centers of   _____
    learning.
    _____

11. Greek cultural influence throughout the Mediterranean area
    weakened after Alexander's death.

12. Economic conditions improved in the Greek city-states after   _____
    Alexander's death.

WORKING WITH MAPS

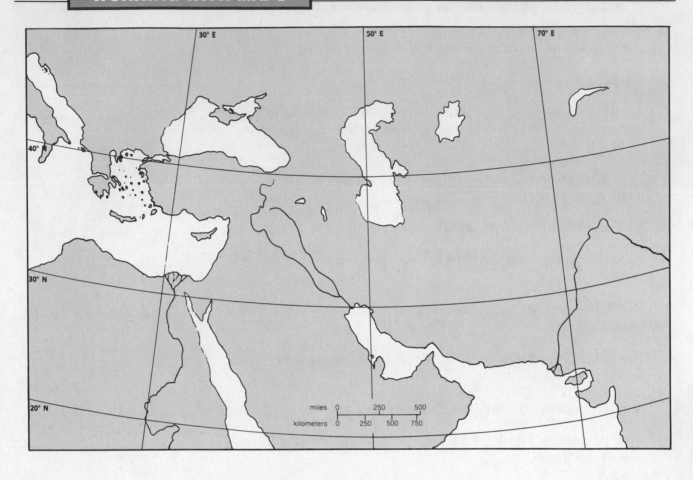

On the map above, label the following: Mediterranean Sea, Caspian Sea, Red Sea, Black Sea, Persian Gulf, Nile River, Indus River, Africa, Asia, India. Draw in the boundaries of Alexander's empire (c. 323 B.C.). Label the various regions it included. Then fill in the blanks below with the names of the places described in the following statements. Label the places on the map. Use dots to show the locations of cities.

_____   1. body of water between Greece and Asia Minor

_____   2. two Greek city-states that tried to stop Philip II's invasion

_____

_____   3. city where Alexander died

_____   4. Hellenistic city known for its intellectual and social life

Geography and History

HUMAN/ENVIRONMENTAL INTERACTION

The places where civilizations grow are often determined by the geographical features that create an environment. Use the map to answer the questions below about human/environmental interaction in ancient Greece.

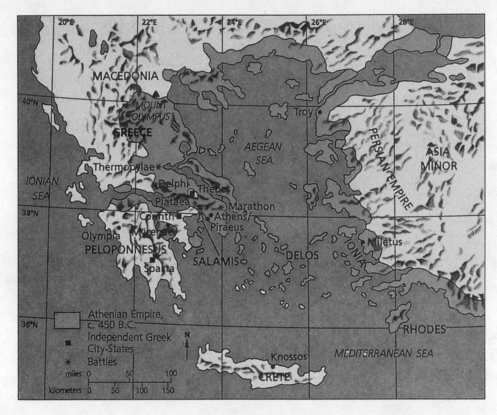

1.   What geographical features influenced the locations of Troy and Miletus? _____

   _____ Which city lay closest to Mount Olympus?_____

2.   Compare the ways of making a living that most likely developed in Corinth and Sparta.

   _____

3.   Which of the Greek city-states was most protected by its location? _____ Why?

   _____

   _____

4.   In what city would you have chosen to settle? _____Why? _____

   _____

UNIT 4 AROUND THE WORLD

THE NUBIANS

Imagine you are reading a newspaper from ancient Greece. The headline presented below might have been used to highlight the accessibility of Nubia during the Ptolemies' rule. Put a check mark by the statements that support the meaning of the headline. Use textbook pages 202–203 to help you complete the page.

NUBIAN TALES FASCINATE GREEK WORLD

___ Few non-Africans had visited Nubia before the Ptolemies.

___ Many Greeks wanted to hunt animals in Nubia.

___ Skilled Nubian archers were famous around the world.

___ Egyptians had told of a rich country south of their country.

___ Kush, a Nubian kingdom, challenged the rule of the Greeks.

Now design a book cover to be used with a book entitled, "Uncovering Nubian Treasures." Use pictures or words to show archaeologists' evidence of the Nubian culture.

Beginnings

FOCUS ON IDEAS

Fill in each blank to form a summary of Chapter 13 by choosing the proper term from the words listed below. Then write the topic of each paragraph in the blank at the beginning of the paragraph.

alphabet	gold	music	soothsayers
arch	Greeks	Palatine	tombs
dancing	landowners	pirates	traders
Etruria	Latins	ritual	women
festivities	Lucius Tarquinius	slaves	workers

1. *Earliest Settlers of Rome*

Rome began as a small settlement on the _____ in central Italy. The first settlers were

_____. Later, the Etruscans settled in the hilly country of _____, north of

Rome. The Etruscans were noted throughout the region as _____ and _____.

They learned much about weapons and battle techniques from the _____.

2. *Etruscan Class System*

The Etruscans were divided into three classes. The upper class consisted of wealthy

_____, nobles, and priests. The middle class was made up of farmers, traders, and

_____, while the lower class was _____.

3. _____

The Etruscans worshiped many gods and used _____ to learn the will of the gods.

They were also concerned about life after death, so they built _____ filled with works

of art and treasures of _____.

4. _____

The Etruscans made many contributions to Roman civilization. They taught the Romans how to

use the _____ in building bridges. The Etruscans also passed on the basics of an

_____ borrowed from the Greeks.

USING VOCABULARY

Chapter 13

Fill in the missing letters of each word below based on the clue provided.

meeting point for the worlds of the living and the dead   m _ n _ u s

public square   _ o _ _ m

underground tombs of the Etruscans   _ a t _ c _ _ b s

parade-like welcome given a Roman hero   t _ i _ m _ h

concerning a city   _ u n _ c i _ a _

Roman games   g _ _ d i _ t o _ i _ l

signs of future events   _ m _ n s

the ways groups of people are classed   s _ _ i a _ o r _ e r

Etruscan cemetery   _ e _ r o p _ l i _

a bundle of rods bound around an axe   f _ _ c _ s

ETRUSCAN CONTRIBUTIONS

The Etruscans made many contributions to Roman civilization. Clues about these contributions are given in the first column. Beside each clue, write the name of the particular contribution to which it refers.

Clue	Contribution
1. Roman amusement	_____
2. writing aid	_____
3. religious ceremony	_____
4. symbol of Roman power	_____
5. parade	_____

Name _____ Date _____ Class _____

CREATE YOUR OWN CITY

The Etruscans and Romans named and laid out their cities according to religious ritual. Imagine yourself as the creator of a new city. Write a legend about how it got its name, and plan a ritual to mark the city's official beginning. Use the lines provided below.

City's Name: _____

Legend: _____

_____

_____

_____

_____

_____

_____

_____

Ritual: _____

_____

_____

_____

_____

_____

_____

_____

_____

Name _____ Date _____ Class _____

WORKING WITH MAPS

A. *Locate and label the following on this map of early Italy: Mediterranean Sea, Tyrrhenian Sea, Adriatic Sea, Po River, Tiber River, Arno River, Corsica, Sardinia, Latium, Etruria, Illyria, Sicily, Caere, and Rome.*

B. *State two reasons the Latins might have founded their city on the Tiber rather than on the Po River.*

_____

_____

_____

_____

Activity Book

The Roman Republic

FOCUS ON IDEAS

Fill in each blank to form a summary of Chapter 14 by choosing the proper term from the words listed below. Then write the topic of each paragraph in the blank at the beginning of the paragraph.

boundaries	generals	legions	Punic Wars
city	Gracchi	Mediterranean	republic
democratic	Italy	Octavian	tribunes
dictatorial	Julius Caesar	Peloponnesian War	triumvirate
economy	latifundias	publicans	Twelve Tables

1. _____

In 509 B.C., the Romans overthrew their Etruscan king and set up a _____. Over the

next 50 years, they took the first steps to a more _____ government. Roman laws were

carved on the _____ _____ so that everyone might see them and know

their rights and duties.

2. _____

Rome gradually expanded and enlarged its _____ until, by 275 B.C., it ruled all of

_____. Rome's well-trained army was organized into _____. Rome

defeated Carthage in the _____ _____. As a result, it became the ruling

power of the _____ region.

3. _____

The conquests had a lasting effect on Rome's _____ and government. Small farms

were replaced by _____, or large estates. Farmers left the land and moved to the

_____. Different leaders tried to solve Rome's problems. The _____broth-

ers gave land to the poor and free grain to the hungry. Soon Roman _____, such as

Marius and Sulla, fought each other for control of the government. In 46 B.C., _____

_____ became ruler of Rome and brought about many reforms. After his death, power

was shared by a(n) _____, or group of three leaders.

USING VOCABULARY

Chapter 14

The alphabetical list contains the letters for spelling the words that complete the statements below. Complete the statements with the proper term and cross out the letters used to spell the answers. When all the statements have been completed, all letters in the alphabetical list will have been used.

A A A A A A A A A B B B B B C C C C C C D D E E E E E E E
F G G I I I I I I I I I I I I I L L L L L L M N N N N N N N
O O O O O O O P P P P R R R R R R R S S S S S S T T T T
T T T U U U U U U U V V V Y

1. What name was given to two elected officials of the Roman Republic who served as administrators and military leaders? _____

2. What word best names things taken from an enemy in war? _____

3. What is a form of government in which the people select their rulers called? _____

4. What were the oldest and wealthiest families of Roman society called? _____

5. What is it called when a vote says "no"? _____

6. What word was the term used by Romans to identify the lower class of people?

    _____

7. Roman soldiers were called _____.

8. What military device did the Romans use successfully on the sea to change a naval battle into a land battle? _____

9. What term was used by Romans to identify their tax collectors? _____.

10. When three rulers share legal powers and make decisions they are called a _____.

11. A person who appoints himself head of a government and has absolute power is called a

    _____.

12. Large estate that produces crops for market is called a _____.

13. The official defender of the lower-class Roman's rights was called a _____.

14. What name was given to a large division of Roman soldiers? _____

WRITING A SPEECH

Imagine that you are Julius Caesar defending your record before the Roman Senate. On the lines below, write a speech stating goals and pointing out accomplishments. Appeal to the senators for support against your opponents.

A. Introduction to Speech

_____

_____

_____

_____

_____

_____

B. Body of Speech

_____

_____

_____

_____

_____

_____

_____

C. Conclusion

_____

_____

_____

_____

_____

_____

WORKING WITH MAPS

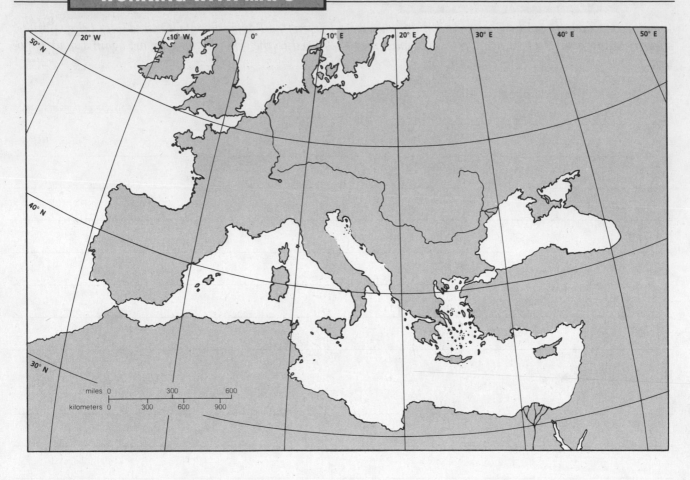

A. On the map above, label the following: *Adriatic Sea, Black Sea, Mediterranean Sea, Atlantic Ocean, Nile River, Egypt, Asia Minor, Greece, Italy, Spain, Gaul, Syria, Rome. Draw in Hannibal's route.*

B. Fill in the blanks below with the names of the places and features described in the statements. Draw and label them on the map.

_____ river that flows through the city of Rome

_____ city that fought Rome in the Punic Wars

_____ island partly controlled by Carthage before the first Punic War

_____ Greek city-state burned by Rome in 146 B.C.

_____ region just north of Greece controlled by Rome

_____ island conquered by Julius Caesar

The Roman Empire

FOCUS ON IDEAS

Fill in each blank to form a summary of Chapter 15 by choosing the proper term from the words listed below. Then write the topic of each paragraph in the blank at the beginning of the paragraph.

Alaric	domus	in town	*Pax Romana*
at home	emperor	increasing prices	politics
Augustus	family	invaders	Praetorian Guard
bathhouses	father	*juris prudentes*	public games
circuses	Germanic invaders	*Pater Patriae*	work
Diocletian	grandfather		

1. _____

Octavian took for himself the title of _____ and became the first _____ of the Roman empire. He brought to the empire a period of peace known as the _____ _____. It lasted for _____ years.

2. _____

In the empire, _____ life was important. The _____ was head of the household. The sons of the poor went to _____, while the sons of the wealthy went to special schools to prepare for careers in _____, philosophy, or medicine. Daughters of the wealthy had lessons _____ _____.

The Roman government staged free _____ public games to entertain the people in the cities. These activities included _____, chariot races, and gladiatorial games. Romans also spent their free time socializing at public _____.

3. _____

By 200 A.D., conditions in the empire worsened. Many emperors were murdered by the army or the _____ _____. People had to pay higher taxes and suffered from _____ _____. The emperors _____ and Constantine I tried to save the empire. However, neither succeeded. The empire faced attacks by _____. In 410 A.D., Rome itself fell to the chief Alaric.

Name _____ Date _____ Class _____

Fill in the squares by spelling out the terms given in the clues below.

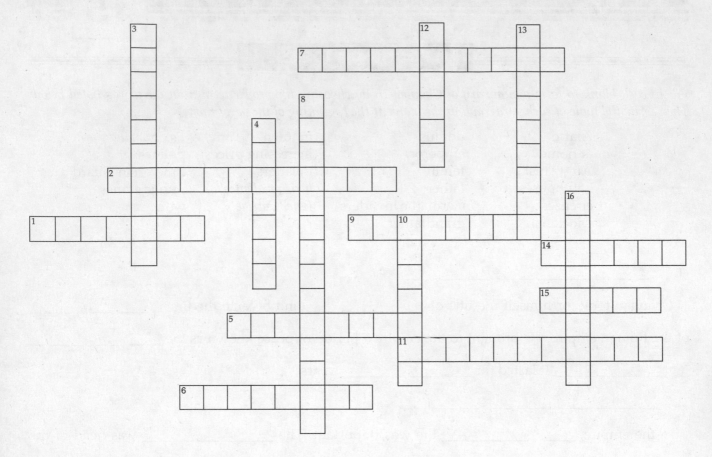

ACROSS
1. absolute ruler of an empire
2. made the same
5. former slaves
6. means "first citizen"
7. type of hunt
9. those who had not paid rent were forced to move out on _____ day
11. ruler's power to rule came from the gods, or rule by _____
14. population count
15. Roman word for home

DOWN
3. people who fought animals or one another in arenas
4. taxes on goods brought into a country
8. lawyers and legal writers who assisted Roman judges
10. Roman apartment houses
12. country estates
13. period of ever-increasing prices
16. speech and writing

EMPIRE IN DECLINE

There were many reasons for the decline and fall of the Roman Empire. Imagine that you are a Roman government leader during the years of the empire's decline. On the lines below, list three steps you might take to save the empire from collapse.

1. _____

   _____

   _____

2. _____

   _____

   _____

3. _____

   _____

SKILL POWER: CRITICAL THINKING

IDENTIFYING THE MAIN IDEA

As you read the following paragraph, ask yourself, "What is the purpose of this paragraph?" Underline the sentences that give supporting details. Identify and circle the sentence that you find to contain the writer's main idea.

PAX ROMANA REVISITED

The peace that Augustus's leadership created for Roman citizens lasted for 200 years. He selected people based on their talent instead of birth and chose to enhance the existing territory rather than conquer more lands. This peaceful environment, without tariffs, gave traders security to travel and build wealth for most sections of the empire. Principles of law that were fair to everyone were developed. Reasonable law brought justice. Everyone was equal before the law and considered to be innocent until proven guilty. As we look at this past and put ancient Roman ideas to work globally, the entire world's future could be a peaceful environment for several centuries.

Write in your own words the main idea of this writer.

_____

_____

_____

_____

WORKING WITH PICTURES

Figures A and B are sketches of two Roman symbols. These symbols represented how the Romans felt about themselves, and how they wanted other countries to view them. Study the sketches to answer the questions below.

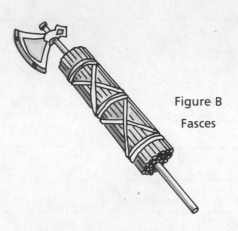

Figure B
Fasces

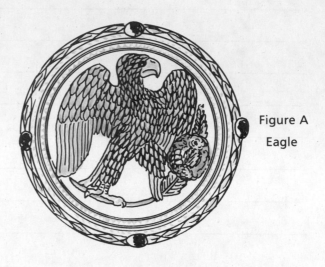

Figure A
Eagle

1.   What is in the center of the bundle of rods in Figure A? _____

2.   In your opinion, what did the Romans want others to understand about them from this symbol?

_____

3.   What is the eagle in Figure B holding in his talons? _____

4.   What characteristics shown in this sketch of the eagle might be desirable in people?

_____

5.   Why do you think modern governments have adopted both of these symbols to use on money

and in government buildings? _____

_____

Name _____ Date _____ Class _____

Christianity

FOCUS ON IDEAS

Fill in each blank to form a summary of Chapter 16 by choosing the proper term from the words listed below. Then write the topic of each paragraph in the blank at the beginning of the paragraph.

Augustine	illegal	monasteries	Pope
Christ	Jewish	New Testament	preaching
Christianity	legal	Old Testament	Romans
government jobs	missionaries	organization	Theodosius

1. _____

Christianity is based on the life and teachings of Jesus, who lived in _____ during the reign of Augustus. Jesus grew up in the town of Nazareth, where he received a _____ education. After three years of _____, he was convicted of treason and was executed on a _____. Soon after his death, Jesus' followers began calling him _____.

2. _____

A Jew named _____ began to preach Christianity throughout the Roman world. After his death, other Christian _____ continued his work. In time, the Roman government made Christianity _____. But, the new religion gained the support of many _____. In 313 A.D., the Edict of Milan made Christianity _____ again. Finally, in 392 A.D., _____ became the official religion of the Roman Empire.

3. _____

The early Christians developed a church _____ and decided what writtings to include in the _____ _____. Religious communities known as _____ and _____ were formed by dedicated Christians. In 1054, the Latin and Greek churches split over the authority of the _____. The Greek churches as a group became known as the _____ _____ Church.

USING VOCABULARY

Column A is a list of coded words, using numbers. Each set of numbers stands for letters of the alphabet. Use the code and the clues to spell each answer in column B. For example, 25, 4, 17, 14, 25, 4 spells church.

1 = __ 2 = __ 3 = __ 4 = __ 5 = __ 6 = __ 7 = __ 8 = __ 9 = __ 10 = __ 11 = __ 12 = __ 13 = __ 14 = __

15 = __ 16 = __ 17 = __ 18 = __ 19 = __ 20 = __ 21 = __ 22 = __ 23 = __ 24 = __ 25 = __ 26 = __

A	Clue	B
26, 5, 11, 25, 1, 15, 1	several parishes grouped together	_____
23, 24, 24, 11, 16	leader of a monastery	_____
23, 12, 11, 15, 16, 8, 1	preacher of Jesus' teachings	_____
9, 1, 15, 15, 5, 23, 4	savior	_____
3, 1, 10, 16, 5, 8, 1, 15	people who are not Jews	_____
9, 5, 15, 15, 5, 11, 10, 23, 14, 21	one who spreads religious beliefs to nonbelievers	_____
15, 25, 14, 5, 12, 16, 17, 14, 1, 15	sacred writings	_____
9, 11, 10, 23, 15,16, 1, 14, 21	Christian settlement	_____
9, 11, 10, 7, 15	male members of a Christian community	_____
4, 1, 14, 1, 15, 21	false teachings	_____
25, 11, 10, 18, 1, 10, 16	a female Christian community	_____
12, 23, 16, 14, 5, 23, 14, 25, 4, 15	five leading archbishops	_____
10, 17, 10, 15	women who lived in separate Christian communities	_____
23, 14, 25, 4, 24, 5, 15, 4, 11, 12, 15	governed Christian churches in large cities	_____
12, 23, 14, 5, 15, 4	a local church area	_____
12, 14, 5, 1, 15, 16	leader of a parish	_____

CORRECT THE STATEMENT

All of the statements below have correct information. Underline the mistake in each statement and write the correction in the space provided.

1. Christianity started among the Jews in Rome. _____

2. Usually only upper-class criminals were executed by crucifixion. _____

3. Paul was the first Christian politician to spread his beliefs to gentiles. _____

4. Early Christians often enjoyed the Roman festivals and games. _____

5. The Edict of Milan made Christianity illegal. _____

6. The Latin and Greek churches split because the Latin churches would not accept the authority of the Pope. _____

7. Monks of Europe helped western civilization survive by taking care of old Greek and Egyptian writings. _____

8. Christians developed a church organization based on the structure of the Hellenistic Empire. _____

9. Jerome translated the Old and New Testaments into Greek. _____

10. Christian writers finally claimed that it was impossible to be both a good Christian and a good Roman. _____

11. Jesus left many written records about his life and teachings. _____

12. Nuns lived in communities known as monasteries. _____

13. A bishop named Augustine suggested that dedicated Christians should form religious communities. _____

14. By 1100 A.D., monks were playing an important role spreading Christianity throughout Europe. _____

WORKING WITH MAPS

Areas can be distinguished on a map using differing colors or shades, or by using a method called hatching. Hatching enables the mapmaker to use a pattern of lines to identify regions.

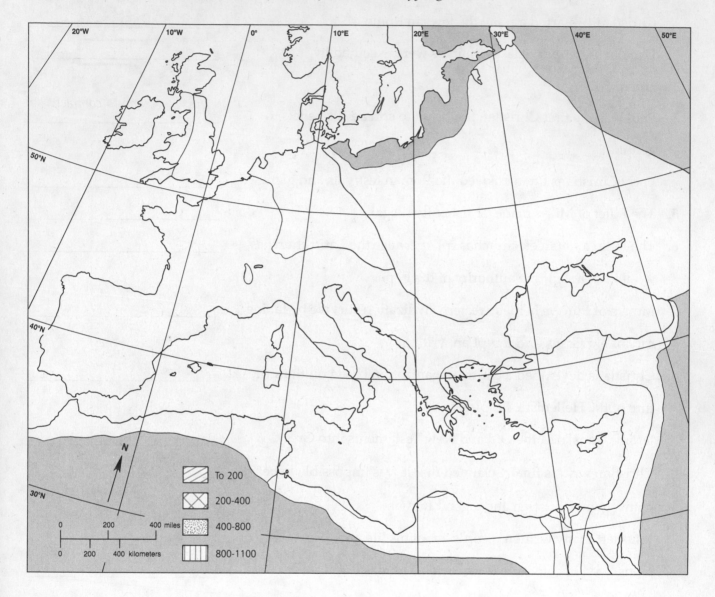

Key:
- To 200
- 200-400
- 400-800
- 800-1100

Use textbook page 251 to help you in your work. Using the key shown above, indicate the spread of Christianity from its beginnings to 1100 A.D. by drawing in the various hatching symbols to show the different time periods.

Geography and History

LOCATING THE ROMAN EMPIRE

Location identifies where a place is exactly and in relation to other places. Use the map below to complete the questions.

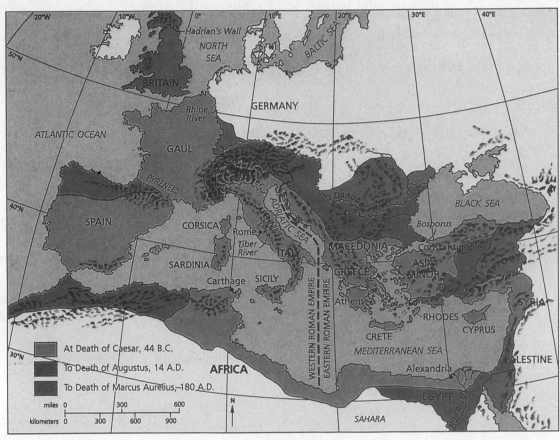

1. Find Rome and the last six territories added to the Roman Empire. What general statements would describe the relative location of Rome and these territories?

   _____

   _____

2. About how far was the distance from Rome to Carthage? _____

   How might knowing this distance help you to explain the early competition between these two

   strong cities? _____

   _____

UNIT 5 — AROUND THE WORLD

THE MOCHE

For each sentence below, choose the correct word or phrase from the list to complete the sentence. Use textbook pages 258–259 to help you complete the page.

1. The Moche rose to power in the _____ deserts of today's Peru.

2. _____ supplied water to turn deserts into farmlands.

3. Information about the Moche culture has been gained from _____ they left behind.

4. The Pyramid of the Sun covered over 12.5 _____.

5. Moche people used the _____ for long-distance trips.

6. We know today how the Moche people looked since they used images of faces to decorate _____.

7. Moche people may have believed in life after death because they filled their graves with a wealth of _____.

8. A powerful group of the Moche were the _____.

9. A population boom occurred among the Moche because even in the desert they were able to produce a great deal of _____.

10. Hundreds of _____ pyramids served as religious and administrative centers.

inland	acres	food
irrigation ditches	coastal	llama
artwork	bottles	pyramids
flat-topped	treasures	warrior-priests

Write a summary statement that explains the importance of religion in the lives of the Moche.

_____

_____

_____

_____

The Germans

FOCUS ON IDEAS

Fill in each blank to form a summary of Chapter 17 by choosing the proper term from the words listed below.

Adrianople	fines	North Africa	ruler
chieftains	government	northern Europe	Spain
cloth	hunting	ordeal	Valhalla
East Goths	kingdoms	people	Vandals
farmlands	loyalty	Persian Empire	West
farm work	Middle Ages	religion	West Goths

1. About 300 A.D., groups of Germans left _____ _____ and settled in the Roman Empire. There, they lived in villages surrounded by _____ and pastures. German men spent most of their time fighting, _____, or making weapons. Women did most of the _____ _____.

2. German warriors were organized into bands headed by _____, who provided the warriors with food and shelter. In return, the warriors gave complete _____. The Germans' love of battle was closely linked to their _____. It was believed that brave warriors who died in battle were carried by goddesses to a place called _____.

3. Germans believed that law came from the _____ and not from a(n) _____. They determined guilt or innocence through _____. German courts often imposed _____ rather than physical punishment or other types of punishment.

4. The _____ _____ defeated the Romans at the battle of _____ in 378 A.D. In 410 A.D., they captured Rome and later moved into _____, where they set up their own kingdom. The _____, another German group, settled in _____ _____ and raided cities and settlements along the coast of the Mediterranean.

USING VOCABULARY

A. *The scrambled words at the beginning of each sentence contain the letters for the two terms needed. Cross off, in order, the letters necessary for the first definition and the term for the second definition will be left.*

T C H U I E N F T I A I C N S

1. Remove a Germanic military leader, _____, and leave _____, garments similar to long shirts.

O A O T R D H E - H A E L P L E R S

2. Remove people who swore that the accused was truthful, or _____-_____, and leave _____, a Germanic method of deciding guilt or innocence.

W B L O E O R D F E G E U D L S D

3. Remove family quarrels, or _____ _____, and leave _____, or fines imposed by Germanic courts.

V A C N L D A A L I N S S M

4. Remove groups based on family ties, or _____, and leave _____, willful destruction of property.

B. *On the lines below, write a brief story using all of the vocabulary words listed above.*

_____

_____

_____

_____

_____

_____

_____

_____

_____

_____

_____

_____

_____

Name _____ Date _____ Class _____

COMPARING THE GERMANS AND THE ROMANS

Germanic people lived within Roman boundaries and adopted some Roman ways of life. However, they still kept much of their own culture. Complete the chart below to compare the two cultures. Then, answer the questions at the bottom.

A.

	Roman Culture	Germanic Culture
Basic religious beliefs	Belief in many gods; religion tied to family life and loyalty to the state; emperor worship.	
Law and government	Organized government of consuls, senators, tribunes, and emperor. Law based on principles decided by judges loyal to the emperor.	
Family life	Family life important. Father headed household and made decisions. Women carried out household chores and enjoyed limited freedom.	
Attitudes toward war	Expansion of empire increased importance of and respect for the army. Generals struggled for political power based on military victories.	

B.

1. How were the Germans like the Romans in their religion? _____

_____

2. What was the basic difference between the two cultures in law and government? _____

_____

3. How were the German people like the Roman people in their family lives? _____

_____

4. What major difference existed in the Germanic attitudes about war and military leaders compared to the Romans? _____

_____

_____

_____

Name _____ Date _____ Class _____

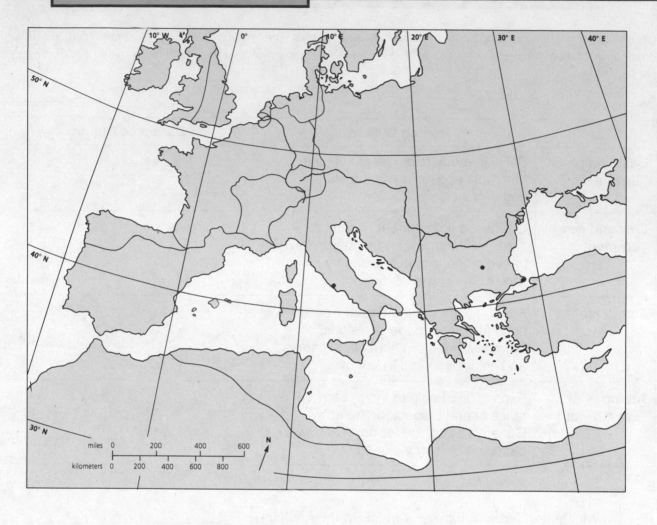

A. *On the map above, label the following: Atlantic Ocean, North Sea, Baltic Sea, Black Sea, Mediterranean Sea, Danube River, Europe, Africa, Italy, Spain, Gaul, Rome, Constantinople, Adrianople, Franks, Ostrogoths, Visigoths, Vandals.*

B. *Study the map to answer the questions below.*

1. What was the importance of Adrianople? _____

_____

2. What is another name on this map for the West Goths? _____

In what country were they located? _____

3. What is another name for the East Goths on this map? _____

In what country were they located? _____

4. What was the general location for the Vandals? _____

Name _____ Date _____ Class _____

The Franks

FOCUS ON IDEAS

Fill in each blank to form a summary of Chapter 18 by choosing the proper term from the words listed below.

arts	France	local	Roman
Catholic	heirs	nobles	schools
Christian	hospitals	official	three
Clovis	Italy	Paris	Tours
dynasty	laws	Pope	weak
four	learning	religion	western Europe

1. During the late 400s, the Franks developed a new civilization that later became the modern nations of _____ and Germany. A king named _____ united all of the Frankish groups under his rule. He set up a capital in _____. He also gained much support by accepting the _____ or _____ religion.

2. Most Frankish kings were _____ rulers. So the Franks turned for leadership to a(n) _____ known as the "Mayor of the Palace." In 732, a mayor named Charles Martel defeated a Muslim army in the Battle of _____. This Frankish victory helped to keep Europe _____.

3. Charles Martel's son Pepin started a new royal _____. Pepin's son Charlemagne created a Christian empire that included most of _____ _____. In 800, the Pope crowned Charlemagne the new _____ emperor.

4. Charlemagne, whose name means "Charles the Great," was a wise and just ruler who issued a variety of _____. He chose officials to take care of _____ problems. The emperor was very interested in _____, and encouraged the Church to found _____ throughout the empire. Under Charlemagne's rule, the _____ began to flourish throughout the empire again.

5. Charlemagne's _____, unfortunately, were unable to hold the empire together. The _____ became increasingly independent. Finally, the empire was divided into _____ kingdoms.

USING VOCABULARY

Unscramble the letters in the first column to spell out the term being described in the second column. Then write the circled letters in the order in which they appear to form the word puzzler at the bottom.

lalowf	not planted	(_)_ _ _ _
dlros	powerful people who were the descendants of Frankish warriors	(_)_ _ _ _
cktsodesa	wooden fences built around the farmhouses of Frankish lords	_ _ _ _ _ _ _ _ _
tecodevrn	to have changed one's religion	(_)_ _ _ _ _ _ _
tscnuo	officials who ran Charlemagne's courts	_ _(_)_ _ _
fssre	people bound to the land	_ _ _ _ _
nitenado	blessed with holy oil	_ _ _(_)_ _ _ _
timnesrls	traveling entertainers	_ _(_)_ _ _ _ _
	??Word Puzzler??	_ _ _ _ _ _ _

SKILL POWER: TECHNOLOGY SKILLS

DEVELOPING MULTIMEDIA PRESENTATIONS

When making a presentation for others, you want them to be interested and to understand. Planning a multimedia presentation requires some decisions to be made. Use textbook page 276 to complete the action steps below.

A. Select a subject or topic _____

B. Highlights included are:

Highlights	Best Media	Tools to Use

C. Two main points that I want my audience to remember are:

_____ reinforced by _____.

_____ reinforced by _____.

CHARLEMAGNE'S SCHOOL

Charlemagne established a school at his palace in Aachen. What was it like to be a student in Charlemagne's palace school? This exercise is designed to help you use your imagination and textbook in finding answers to this question.

A. *Read the following statements. Then write your answer to each statement in the space provided. In some cases, you may wish to do a diagram or draw a picture for your answer.*

1. Your name

2. Father's name and occupation

3. Teacher's name

4. Subjects taught at school

5. Form of writing used

6. Type of school dress

7. Appearance of classroom

B. *Pretend that Charlemagne is visiting the palace school. One the lines below, write about your impressions of his visit. Describe the emperor's appearance and actions. Mention a question he might have asked the teachers and students about learning.*

_____

_____

_____

_____

_____

_____

_____

_____

WORKING WITH MAPS

In the following exercise, a map legend, scale, and directional arrow are given. In the space provided, draw your impression of a Frankish estate and surroundings using the symbols given. Use your textbook, pages 283-285, to assist you.

N ↑

Title

0   10 miles

Legend

Lake	Oats/Barley Field	Noble's House
Stream	Wheat/Rye Field	Stockade
Trail	Fallow Field	Chapel
Main Road	Pasture	Farmer's House
Forest	Orchard	Vineyard

The Irish and The Anglo-Saxons

FOCUS ON IDEAS

Fill in each blank to form a summary of Chapter 19 by choosing the proper term from the words listed below. Then write the topic of each paragraph in the blank at the beginning of the paragraph.

abbots	Celts	England	missionary
Alfred	Christianity	farm	Romans
Anglo-Saxons	converts	Germanic	Saint Columba
Augustine	Danelaw	Gregory I	Saint Patrick
Celtic	Danes	Ireland	Saxons

1. _____

   The _____ ruled Britain for nearly 400 years. They, however, did not win over the conquered people known as the _____. In 410, Britain was invaded by groups from northern Germany and Denmark called Angles, _____, and Jutes. Together, they became known as _____. The southern part of Britain in which they settled was called _____.

2. _____

   During this period, Ireland became the major center of _____ culture. Irish scholars and artists were strongly influenced by _____. The Irish Church was founded in the 400s by _____. Irish monks did _____ work and sailed the North Atlantic in search of new _____.

3. _____

   Pope _____ decided to win the Germanic kingdoms in Britain to Christianity. In 597, he sent a mission of monks led by _____ to England. By 700, all England was Christian. In the 800s, bands of _____ conquered areas of England. The English kingdoms eventually united under King _____ to hold back the conquerors. In later years, the English took control of the conquered territory known as _____ and made it a part of their kingdom.

Name _____ Date _____ Class _____

On the left is a list of clues to the coded words in the middle. To decode the words, substitute letters of the alphabet for the letters in each set. Use each clue and its code to spell the answer. For example, A J A K Z spells Irish.

A =__ B =__ C =__ D =__ E =__ F =__ G =__ H =__ I =__ J =__ K =__ L =__ M =__

N =__ 0 =__ P =__ Q =__ R =__ S =__ T =__ U =__ V =__ W =__ X =__ Y =__ Z =__

1. woven hanging in a noble's home   L S H W K L J Q   _____

2. royal protection   C A F Y ' K   H W S U W   _____

3. Irish boats   U G J S U D W K   _____

4. a wise man, or member of the witenagemot   O A L S F   _____

5. an English government district   K Z A J W   _____

6. council of nobles and church leaders   O A L W F S Y W E G L   _____

7. most important work in Anglo-Saxon literature   T W G O M D X   _____

8. local noble chosen by the king to control a district   K Z W J A X X   _____

9. early name for England   S F Y D W D S F V   _____

STUDYING ENGLISH HISTORY

This chart shows major events and dates in English history. In the spaces provided, fill in the results or outcome of each event.

Date	Event	Result
410	Roman legions left Britain	
597	Pope Gregory sent monks from Rome to England	
700	All England became Christian	
835	Danes attacked and settled in England	
878	Danes were defeated, but not driven out of England	

UNDERSTANDING PASSAGES

Read the following passage written by St. Augustine. Then check the statement in each pair that expresses the ideas in the passage.

Men will not do what is right, either because the right is hidden from them or because they find no delight in it. But that what was hidden may become clear, what delighted not may become sweet—this belongs to the grace of God.

A. ___ People do not do what is right because of two reasons.

B. ___ People do not do what is right because of many reasons.

A. ___ We can never know if what we do is right.

B. ___ The right way becomes known through the grace of God.

A. ___ People always find delight in truth and right.

B. ___ Some people find no delight in truth and right.

A. ___ A person who cannot distinguish right will never be able to distinguish it.

B. ___ A person who cannot distinguish right may do so someday.

WORKING WITH MAPS

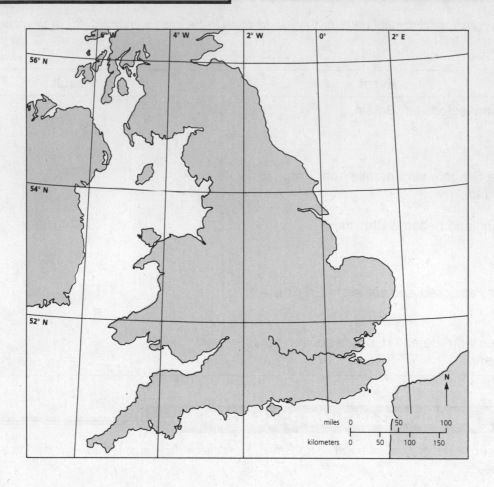

A. *On the map above, label the following: Atlantic Ocean, North Sea, Irish Sea, English Channel, Celtic Ireland, Thames River, Iona, Kent, Wessex, Canterbury, and London. Draw in the borders for the Danelaw and label it.*

B. *Fill in the blanks below with the names of the places described in the statements.*

_____ island off the west coast of Scotland where Saint Columba set up a monastery as a base for missionaries

_____ city where Augustine built a Christian church

_____ city rebuilt by Alfred after it was partly destroyed by Danes

_____ small kingdom that was the home of Alfred

_____ kingdom of Ethelbert and Bertha

The Vikings

FOCUS ON IDEAS

Fill in each blank to form a summary of Chapter 20 by choosing the proper term from the words listed below. Then write the topic of each paragraph in the blank at the beginning of the paragraph.

attacked	gods	North America	sailors
different	isolated	overcrowded	Scandinavia
Eddas	magic charms	road markers	Swedish
France	market	Roman	Varangian Route
German	Norsemen	runes	warriors

1. _____

During the 900s, the Vikings, or _____, sailed from their homeland and attacked Charlemagne's empire and Anglo-Saxon England. These people were excellent _____. They were also skilled _____ who opened up new trade routes. Trade led to the growth of _____ towns. But, most Vikings lived in villages that were _____ from one another.

2. _____

The Vikings told stories about the deeds of their _____. Later, these stories became written poems called _____. The Viking language developed into four separate languages—Danish, _____, Norwegian, and Icelandic. They were written with letters called _____. When they accepted Christianity, the Vikings began to write their languages with _____ letters.

3. _____

By the end of the 800s, many Viking villages were _____. Many Viking warriors left their homes in _____ and traveled the coasts and rivers of Europe. Swedish Vikings established the _____ _____ from the Baltic Sea to Byzantium. Norwegian Vikings sailed as far west as _____ _____. The Danish Vikings settled in areas of England and _____.

USING VOCABULARY

Write a complete definition for each vocabulary word listed below. Then, match each vocabulary word with the correct picture on the right by placing the letter of the picture after the proper definition in the blank provided. Where none is provided, draw a sketch of the vocabulary word.

berserkers _____ _____ _____ ___		**A**
fjords _____ _____ _____		**B**
runes _____ _____ _____ ___		**C**
bonfire _____ _____ _____ ___		**D**
dragon's head _____ _____ _____		**E**
jarl _____ _____ _____		**F**

VIKING STORYTELLING

The Vikings taught their children stories about their gods and heroes. Below is a version of the tale, "Odin Goes to Mimir's Well." Read the tale to discover the main ideas. Then, answer the question that follows the tale.

Odin, the chief Norse god, found out that the world was full of trouble and sorrow. He felt that if he were wiser, he could help the world's people. So he decided to drink from Mimir's well, where wisdom was stored.

Disguised as a wanderer, Odin started on his long journey to the well. On the way, he met the Wise Giant, who guarded the entrance to the well. The giant refused to admit anyone to the well who did not know the special secret. Odin did not know the secret, but he was sure he could persuade the giant to give it to him.

Odin asked the giant to join him in a debate to prove who was smarter. The winner would receive the loser's head. The giant agreed, and he and Odin debated all day long. Finally, Odin won. To save his head, the giant told Odin the secret—to drink from Mimir's well, a price had to be paid. The price was the loss of an eye.

Odin, afraid of the pain he would have to suffer, almost turned back. But then he thought about his responsibility to the world. So he went to the well, where he met Mimir. Mimir recognized Odin and told him no one had ever paid the price for a drink. When Odin said he would pay it, Mimir gave him a big drink from the well.

As Odin drank, the future became clear to him. He saw that by living good lives, people could destroy the evil that caused problems. When he finished his drink, Odin plucked out his right eye. Mimir threw the eye to the bottom of the well, where it remained as a permanent reminder of the cost of wisdom.

What lessons would Viking children learn from this story?

_____

_____

_____

_____

_____

_____

_____

_____

_____

_____

_____

_____

Name _____ Date _____ Class _____

Below is a diagram of a Viking warship. Study the diagram and use your text to answer the questions at the bottom of the page.

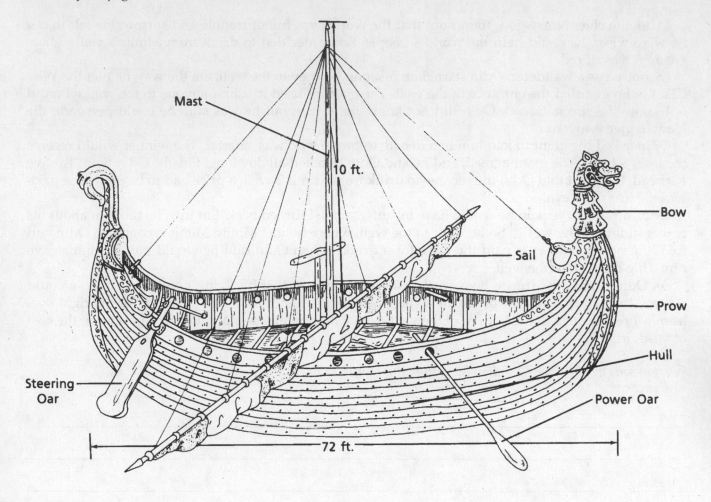

1. What propelled a Viking warship on the oceans or sea? _____

_____

2. Where might the power oars be used? _____

3. Why did the Vikings carve the tall bow in the shape of a dragon's head? _____

_____

4. Why did the Vikings turn to the sea for a living? _____

_____

5. In your opinion, what might be the nature of the people who decided to travel in this ship out on

the open sea? _____

_____

Geography and History

UNIT
6

UNDERSTANDING PLACE : HUMAN CHARACTERISTICS

Use the information in Unit Six to complete the comparison chart below about the human characteristics of the Early Middle Ages. Then, use your chart and the maps in Unit 6 of your text to answer the following questions.

Country	Germanic	Franks	Irish/Anglo-Saxons	Vikings
How They Made a Living	cattle herders traders farmers warriors		sailors farmers priests	
Religion		accepted Christianity early		believed gods responsible for weather and crop growth, sagas about gods' deeds
Kinds of Government	military chieftains were leaders; laws came from people			no central government; led by *jarls* or military chieftains
Need for Expansion	love of battle		Ireland was Celtic culture. Anglo-Saxons were united under Alfred.	

1. Which people seem to have the most urgent need to find additional land? Why? _____

   _____

2. What geographic features caused the need for expansion for the country you named in question 1?

   _____

   _____

3. How might a German's explanation of why crops had failed be different than an Anglo-Saxons

   explanation for the same thing? _____

   _____

Name _____ Date _____ Class _____

THE GUPTAS

Imagine you are a reporter from ancient India. Your assignment is to write an article about the Golden Age of India. The editor has given you three areas of content to cover—culture, empire expansion, and unification efforts. Use the notes in the box to outline your reporting. Begin your article with a topic sentence. Use textbook pages 310–311 to help you complete the page.

> • new numbering system developed
> • Hinduism declared dominant religion
> • expansion brings profitable trading
> • Guptas appreciate conquest
> • art flourishes
> • Monks honor Buddha in sculpture

GOLDEN AGE OF INDIA

By _____

Reporter's Name

_____

_____

Culture _____

_____

_____

Empire Expansion _____

_____

_____

Unification Efforts _____

_____

_____

The future world will remember the Gupta Empire best for _____

_____

_____

The Byzantine Empire

FOCUS ON IDEAS

Fill in each blank to form a summary of Chapter 21 by choosing the proper term from the words listed below.
Then write the topic of each paragraph in the blank at the beginning of the paragraph.

Belisarius	Germany	Kievan Rus	territory
Byzantine	Hagia Sophia	law code	Theodora
Christ	icons	patriarch	Turkish
Constantine	Justinian	Pope	united

1. _____

About 330, the Emperor _____ moved the capital of the Roman Empire from Rome to Constantinople. This eastern Roman Empire became known as the _____ Empire. Its ideas and practices later shaped the development of _____ _____ and other Eastern European countries.

2. _____

In 527, a general named _____ became the Byzantine emperor. He and his wife, _____, cooperated in the government and were strong rulers. One of the emperor's achievements was a _____ _____ that influenced the legal system of western countries. He also built the _____ _____, the religious center of the empire.

3. _____

Church and government were _____ in the Byzantine Empire. It was believed that emperors, who were all-powerful, were representatives of _____. The leading church official was the _____ of Constantinople. Between 726 and 843, church leaders argued over the use of _____.

4. _____

Disputes between the Byzantines and the _____ led to a final split between eastern and western Christianity in 1054. Due to outside invaders, the Byzantine Empire lost much of its _____. In 1453, _____ armies captured Constantinople.

USING VOCABULARY

Chapter 21

The alphabetical list contains the letters for spelling the words that answer the exercises below. Complete the exercises with the proper word(s), and cross out the letters used to spell the answers. When all of the exercises have been completed, all letters in the alphabetical list will have been used.

A A C C C C C D E E E E E F G G H I I I I I I K L L L M M N N
O O O O O O O P R R R R R R S S S S S T T T W Y Y Y

1.   What is a religious image used in worship called?_____

2.   What is the name of the gift (goods, money, or property) that a woman in earlier times brought

to her marriage? _____

3.   Name the first secret weapon—a chemical mixture that ignited when in contact with water.

_____ _____

4.   Eastern Orthodox church officials were called _____.

5.   What term is used to name valued holy objects from the past? _____

6.   What was the name of the alphabet given to the Slavs? _____

7.   What are pictures called that are made up of many bits of colored glass or stone? _____

8.   Name the word for the study of religion. _____

SKILL POWER: CRITICAL THINKING

MAKING GENERALIZATIONS

To practice this skill, read the supporting sentences given for each mystery topic. Identify the subject in the space provided. Use textbook pages 317–319 to help you complete the page.

Mystery Topic _____

- It took four years to build.
- Protection was provided by the sea on three sides.
- Its political and social life mirrored Rome.
- The location was at the crossroads of sea and land trade.

Write a generalization about this topic.

_____

_____

Mystery Topic _____

- The largest buildings were churches.
- Byzantines believed that each person was responsible for the well-being of all people.
- Needy people were given assistance.
- It was dedicated to God.

Write a generalization about this topic.

_____

_____

BYZANTINE NEWS STORIES

Imagine that you are the editor of the Constantinople Times and that you are writing news stories about important Byzantine events. The boxes below contain news headlines from Byzantine history. In the empty space provided in each box, write one or two sentences that might appear in an article describing the headline.

330 A.D.

CONSTANTINE FOUNDS
NEW CAPITAL

532 A.D.

THEODORA OPPOSES
REVOLT

726 A.D.

LEO III FORBIDS USE
OF ICONS

1453 A.D.

TURKS CAPTURE
CONSTANTINOPLE

Name _____ Date _____ Class _____

Study the map of the Byzantine Empire below and complete the activity that follows. You may need to use the text, Chapter 21, to help you with some of the answers.

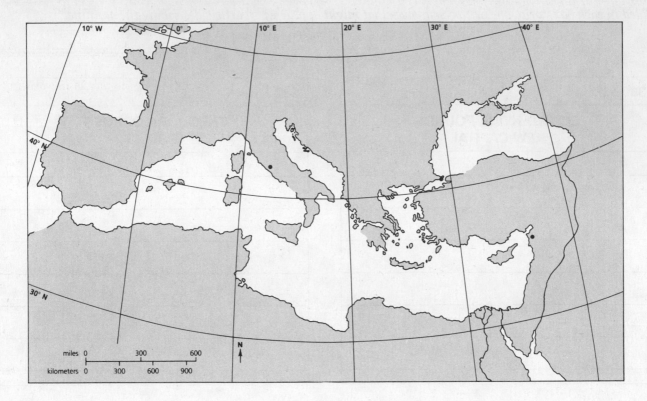

1.   Locate and label the following on the map: Mediterranean Sea, Aegean Sea, Black Sea, Atlantic Ocean, Italy, Antioch, Rome, Constantinople, Vandals, Franks, and Visigoths.

2.   Outline the borders of the Byzantine Empire including the areas conquered by Justinian up to 565.

3.   Place an X in the blanks provided if the peoples or cities listed were within the area of the Byzantine Empire under Justinian.

Antioch   _____   Franks   _____

Constantinople   _____   Visigoths   _____

Vandals   _____   Rome   _____

The Spread of Islam

FOCUS ON IDEAS

Fill in each blank to form a summary of Chapter 22 by choosing the proper term from the words listed below. Then write the topic of each paragraph in the blank at the beginning of the paragraph.

Abbasids	empire	moat	Tá if
algebra	equal	Mu'awiya	taxes
Allah	geometric	Muhammad	trade
Arabia	Islam	Persians	vizier
Arabic	Ka'bah	religion	Yahweh
caliph	Makkah	Spain	

1. _____

   In the 600s, a new religion called _____ appeared in the mountainous area of western _____. It was based on the preaching of a prophet named _____. He proclaimed as stated in the Quaran that the only god was _____, before whom all believers were _____. In time, the city of _____ became the center of the new religion.

2. _____

   After the death of the prophet, a leader was chosen called a(n) _____. Arabs succeeded in conquering a large _____. In 661, a ruler called _____ moved the capital to Damascus and founded the Umayyad dynasty. The government was reorganized, and _____ was made the official language. The Arab Empire expanded into central Asia, North Africa, and most of _____. In 750, the _____ took control and built a new capital at Baghdad. This new dynasty concentrated on _____ rather than war. However, in 945, the _____ took control.

3. _____

   From the eighth to the fourteenth centuries, the Arabs made important contributions to modern civilization. Arab mathematicians invented _____ and introduced it to the Europeans. The Arabs excelled in medicine. They also made many contributions in the arts. Mosques and other buildings were decorated with distinct and colorful _____ designs.

USING VOCABULARY   **Chapter 22**

Fill in the squares by spelling out the terms given in the clues below.

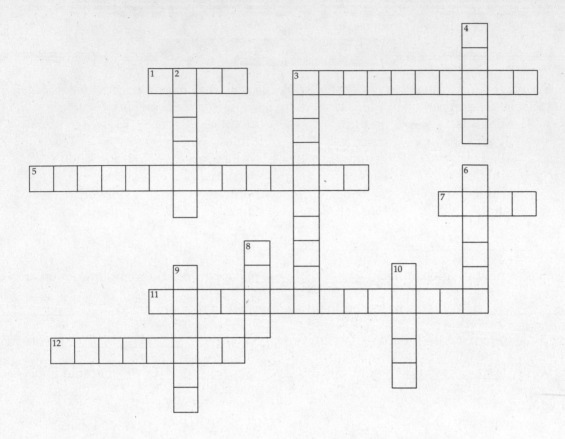

ACROSS
1. Muslim prayer leader
3. means "year of migration"
5. a time when the dead will rise up to be judged
7. journey to Makkah
11. five required Muslim duties
12. travelers to a religious shrine

DOWN
2. Islamic place of worship
3. scientists who used magic and chemistry to try to make gold and silver
4. Muslim scriptures
6. Muslim leader
8. wide ditch filled with water
9. adviser to Abbasid ruler
10. charity

CREATING MESSAGES

Have you ever noticed billboards with religious messages on them? Suppose you wanted to let people know more about the life and beliefs of Muhammad. How may you achieve this aim using billboards? In the four boxes below, create your own messages. Briefly write or sketch in each box information about these four themes in the life of Muhammad: his early life and the revelation, the religious ideas that he preached, the beginning of Islam, and his eventual success in Makkah.

1

2

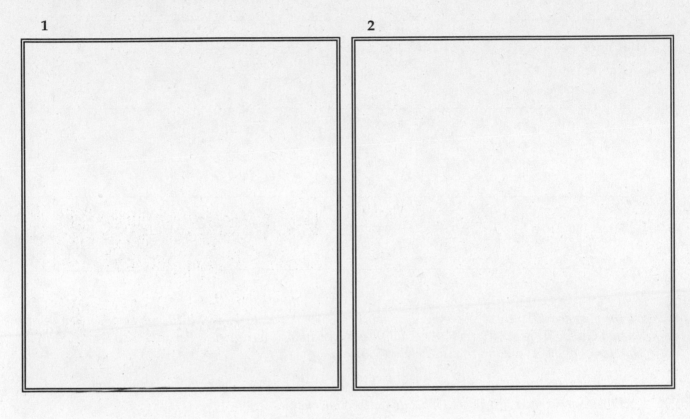

3

4

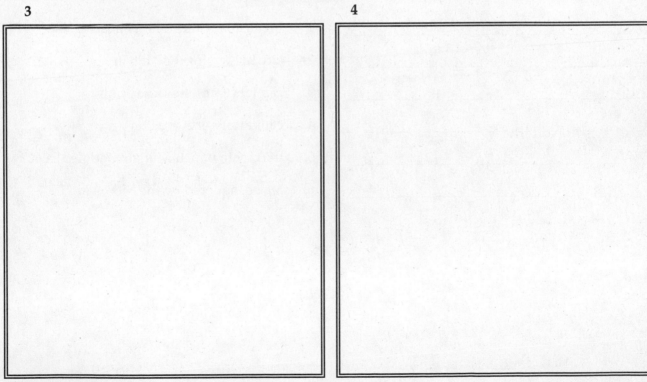

WORKING WITH MAPS

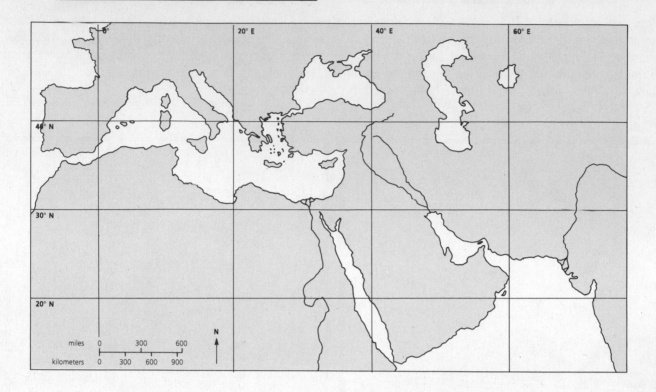

A. On the map above, label the following: *Arabian Sea, Caspian Sea, Red Sea, Mediterranean Sea, Black Sea, Persian Gulf, Nile River, Tigris River, Euphrates River, Indus River, Africa, Persia, India. Draw in the boundaries of the Arab Empire at its height (750).*

B. *Fill in the blanks below with the names of the places and features described in the sentences. Draw and label them on the map. Use dots to indicate the location of cities.*

_____ 1. peninsula where Islam began

_____ 2. city known for the Ka'bah

_____ 3. capital city of the Umayyads

_____ 4. capital city of Abbasids

_____ 5. the city to which Muhammad fled in 622

_____ 6. area conquered by the Moors in 710

The Eastern Slavs

Chapter 23

FOCUS ON IDEAS

Fill in each blank to form a summary of Chapter 23 by choosing the proper term from the words listed below. Then write the topic of each paragraph in the blank at the beginning of the paragraph.

Black Sea	czar	Kiev	the Terrible
boyars	disorder	Mongols	Varangians
Byzantine	Eastern Christianity	north	villages
Caspian Sea	farming	south	Vladimir I
collection	Ivan III	the Great	Volga

1. _____

Between 500 and 800, Eastern Slavs settled in forested land west of the _____ River.

They established villages and cleared the land. The land, animals, and tools belonged to the

_____ rather than to individuals. Before long, merchants set up a trade route that ran

from the Baltic Sea in the north to the _____ _____ in the south.

2. _____

Viking warriors known as _____ protected the weak trading towns. A

_____ of small territories was headed by the Grand Prince of _____. One of

its first strong rulers was _____. In 988, he chose _____ _____

as the official religion. As a result, _____ culture influenced the early development of

Kievan Rus.

3. _____

Around 1240, the _____ took control. Many Rus people moved _____

and settled near Moscow. In 1480, a prince of Moscow, _____, ended foreign control.

He became very powerful and called himself _____. His grandson Ivan IV enlarged

their borders and became known as "_____ _____." After Ivan's IV's

death, Muscovy entered a period of _____.

USING VOCABULARY

Write a complete definition for each vocabulary word listed below. Then, match each vocabulary word with the correct picture on the right by placing the letter of the picture after the proper definition in the blank provided. Where none is provided, draw a sketch of the vocabulary word.

A

izba _____

_____

_____

B

_____ open grasslands of Kievan Rus _____

_____

_____

C

_____ a noble who owned land; assisted Grand Prince of Kiev

_____

_____

D

khan _____

_____

_____

E

kremlin _____

_____

_____

F

caftan _____

_____

_____

WRITING A RÉSUMÉ

When you try to get your first paying job, your employer may ask you for a résumé. This is a brief, written description of your background, experiences, and past achievements. A good résumé may get you an interview and possibly the job. Your textbook reading describes the life of Ivan the Terrible. Imagine that Ivan has been defeated by his enemies, that he is forced to flee, and that he has to get a job while out of the country. How would he write his résumé if he wanted to become ruler of another land?

Résumé of Ivan the Terrible

Job ambition: _____

_____

Family background: _____

_____

Early work experience: _____

_____

_____

_____

Great achievements: _____

_____

_____

_____

_____

Strong points in personality and character: _____

_____

_____

_____

References of people who know my abilities: _____

_____

_____

_____

Name _____ Date _____ Class _____

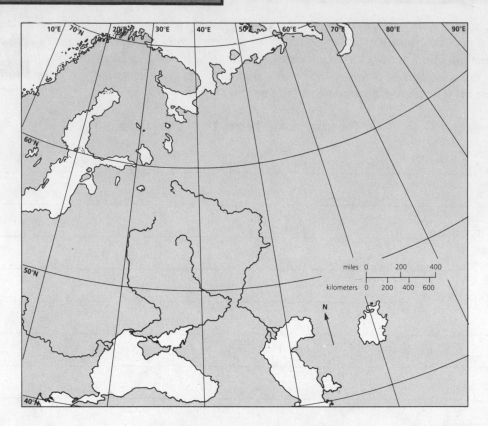

A. On the map above, label the following: Baltic Sea, Black Sea, Caspian Sea, Arctic Ocean, Danube River, Dnieper River, Don River, Europe, Norway, Sweden, Siberia, Ottoman Empire. Draw in the border for the Grand Principality of Moscow in 1300. Then, draw in the boundaries for Muscovy in 1584.

B. Fill in the blanks below with the names of the places and features described. Label them on the map.

_____   1. river near which the Eastern Slavs settled

_____   2. town ruled by Rurik

_____   3. capital of the first Rus state

_____   4. center of the Rus branch of the Eastern Orthodox Church

_____   5. land attacked by Muscovite armies in 1558

Geography and History

THE GROWTH OF MOSCOW

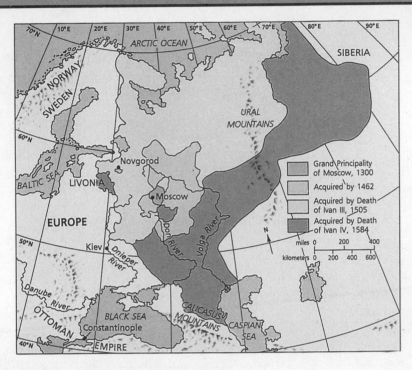

Noting the location of the Muscovites in their world will help us to understand more about lives they led. Study the map provided below to complete the questions at the bottom of the page.

1. Locate the following cities by latitude and longitude:

   Moscow   Latitude _____   Longitude _____

   Kiev   Latitude _____   Longitude _____

2. What two rivers were important to the Rus people? _____ Which of

   these rivers was more important to the growth of Moscow? _____

3. What is the relationship of location of the Black Sea to Moscow? _____

   _____

   Why was this important to the people of Moscow? _____

   _____

4. Between what two lines of latitude were the three cities in Rus territories located? _____

   _____

UNIT 7 AROUND THE WORLD

THE ANASAZI

A. *Fill in the blanks below with the correct term or name. Use textbook pages 360–361 to help you complete the page.*

1. _____ current name of the area where the Anasazi lived

2. _____ a stone that has many color shades of green to blue

3. _____ large circular underground chambers

4. _____ apartment complex-like houses built in Mesa Verde

5. _____ messages left in picture form

6. _____ Spanish word for villages

B. *Explain why we believe the Anasazi built an advanced culture in North America from approximately 200 A.D. to 1300 A.D. Use all of the phrases given at the bottom of the page. You may add other information to complete your explanation.*

_____

_____

_____

_____

_____

_____

- evidence of trade with civilizations in Mexico and Central America

- network of trails and roads—some more than 30 feet wide

- like modern apartment houses

- Pueblo trace their heritage back to the Anasazi

Feudal Society

FOCUS ON IDEAS

Fill in the blanks to form a summary of Chapter 24. You will find some of the proper terms listed below. For other words, you may need to use your textbook.

castle	enlarged	kings	military service
central	fief	loyalty	money payments
duty	five	merchants	peasants
emperors	horseback	methods	serfs

During the Middle Ages, western Europe had no_____ government to keep the peace. _____ were weak and depended on nobles for food, horses, and soldiers. The nobles owned much of the _____ and became independent rulers. They raised their own _____ and enforced the law in their territories.

A more complex system of government developed known as _____. It was based on strong feelings of _____ and _____ among all nobles. A vassal gave _____. In return, the lord promised to protect his vassal and gave him an estate called a(n) _____. Almost all nobles were knights, or warriors on _____. A noble began his training for knighthood at the _____ of a great lord. If he proved to be a good fighter, a young noble was made a knight in a ceremony known as _____.

Most people were _____ who worked the land. The land was divided into _____, or farming communities. A group known as _____ were bound to the land. They spent three days of the week working in the lord's fields. Another group, known as freemen, paid _____. By the 1200s, better farming _____ were used. As a result, fields were _____ and more food was grown.

USING VOCABULARY

Read the clues given and write the correct word or phrase on the line before its clue. Then, find and circle the 22 words and 2 phrases in the puzzle. The words in the puzzle are spelled horizontally, vertically, in backward order, or around corners.

Word or Phrase | **Clue**

_____ people who worked the land or served the nobles

_____ pledge of loyalty given by a vassal to a lord

_____ high wooden fence

_____ special contest for knights

_____ religious leaders

_____ war-horses

_____ contest of strength using blunt lances

_____ peasants who paid the lord for the right to farm the land

_____ a farming community

_____ an official who made sure the peasants worked hard

_____ ceremony to become a knight

_____ teenager training for knighthood

_____ noblewomen

_____ tall castle tower

_____ rules for knights

_____ sword holder

_____ official who looked after the lord's fiefs

_____ noble who served a lord or higher rank

_____ feudal estates

_____ government by land-owning nobles

_____ fortress built of stone

_____ heavy iron gate

_____ warriors on horseback

_____ a very young boy who helped the knights

A V L A D I E S C O D E O F C H I V A L R Y F I E F F R

S S A L C A R T S B A I L I F F S I L L U

E E M E N F E U D A L I S M E J O A N D R B Y H B H D R

K K N I G H T S S T N A S A E P C L E R

G Y S E N E S C H A L C A S T L

E E P E D A S I L A P E

P S R E I R T

A G E

S E D T S U O J

O T O U R N A M E N T K

C T R O P M A N O R G N I B B U D O P L E H E

E R I U Q S R O S E S A C T O F H O M A G E T S C A B B A

SEPARATING FACT FROM OPINION

Read each of the following statements about feudal society and decide whether it is a fact or opinion. In the space provided, write "O" for opinion and "F" for fact.

_____ **1.** Cooperation was important in feudal life.

_____ **2.** Feudalism was an excellent way to organize a society.

_____ **3.** Nobles protected their estates.

_____ **4.** Feudal society consisted of nobles, clergy, peasants, and townspeople.

_____ **5.** The nobles were the most important group in feudal times.

_____ **6.** The peasants lived on manors.

Name _____ Date _____ Class _____

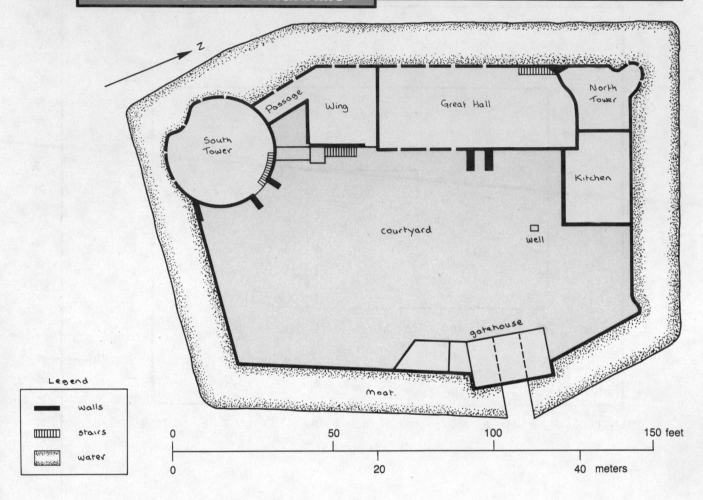

Legend

▬ walls

▥ stairs

▧ water

During the Middle Ages, castles served as both homes and fortresses for the nobility. Use the diagram of the castle to answer the following questions.

1. In what part of the castle might the lord and his family live?_____

_____

2. In what part would the large feasts be held? _____

3. In times of attack where might the guards be stationed? _____

_____

4. Where might the serfs or peasants work in this castle? _____

_____

5. If you were a spy against the lord, how would you use this plan to assist your work? _____

_____

6. How wide is the Great Hall? _____

   How long is it? _____

The Church

FOCUS ON IDEAS

Fill in the blanks to form a summary of Chapter 25. You will find some of the proper terms listed below. For other words, you may need to use your textbook.

cathedral	feudalism	peasants	trade
civilization	ideal	permanent	united
customs	kings	Roman Empire	universities
failure	nobles	Saladin	Urban II

The Roman Catholic Church was the only organization that _____ western Europeans during the Middle Ages. Church leaders wanted to build a(n) _____ based on Christian principles. They helped to preserve and pass on the heritage of the _____ _____. Parish clergy set up _____ schools in towns to educate the people. By the 1200s, _____ grew from these schools and spread throughout Europe. Scholars, such as Thomas Aquinas, tried with their writings_____

_____.

In 1701, _____ _____ conquered Jerusalem and threatened the Byzantine Empire. Pope _____ finally agreed to help the Byzantines and to regain the Holy Land. In 1095, he called on the people and the leaders of western Europe to _____

_____. One year later, a large group of _____ started a crusade, but were almost completely wiped out by the Turks. European _____ set out on a well-organized crusade and finally, after a long march, they _____. Many crusaders stayed in Palestine, where they set up four feudal kingdoms called _____.

In 1187, the Muslim leader _____ took Jerusalem from the crusaders. Another crusade was organized and led by the English, French, and German _____. It proved to be a(n) _____. King _____ of England fought the Muslims for three years, but could not defeat them.

Name _____ Date _____ Class _____

In 1202, another group of crusaders, with the aid of _____ merchants, fought the Byzantines instead of the Muslims. They seized _____ and ruled it for nearly 60 years. As a result of this crusade, many western Europeans lost respect for the crusader _____. By 1291, the Muslims had gained back all the land in _____ that the crusaders had earlier captured.

The Crusades had several important effects. One was that the split between eastern and western Christianity became _____. Also, the Crusades helped to break down _____, and encouraged the growth of _____ and towns in western Europe.

SKILL POWER: TECHNOLOGY SKILL

USING THE INTERNET

Fill in the blanks below with the correct term or name about using the Internet. Words in the box will help you. Use textbook page 390 to help you complete the page.

1. _____ a global computer network

2. _____ a company that charges you a fee to enter the Internet

3. _____ a program that lets you explore information on the World Wide Web

4. _____ an electronic machine that performs high-speed processes

5. _____ a device that lets your computer send and receive data by telephone

6. _____ to skim through an electronic "world" to seek information

7. _____ a Web page address

8. _____ enter a personal password for access to the Internet

9. _____ interconnected computer documents that contain information

10. _____ a space in the World Wide Web created for a specific topic

modem	Internet	service provider	World Wide Web
computer	Web browser	surf	Uniform Resource Locator (URL)
log on	Web site		

USING VOCABULARY

Chapter 25

Fill in the squares by spelling out the terms given in the clues below.

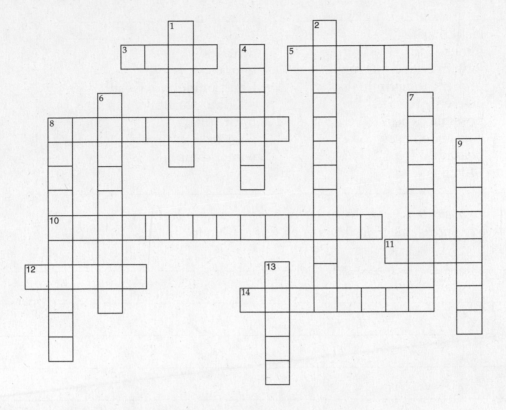

ACROSS

3. Muslim military leader
5. groups of people joined for a common cause
8. church official who headed a university
10. to have lost church membership
11. worship service
12. group of friars
14. series of holy wars that lasted about 200 years

DOWN

1. church offerings equal to 10 percent of a person's income
2. groups of people devoted to learning
4. deeply religious
6. killed
7. laws set up by the Church
8. churches headed by bishops
9. weapon used to fire an arrow with great force
13. traveling preacher

BEING CREATIVE: WHAT'S IT LIKE TO BE A CRUSADER?

Imagine that you are a student in a German high school. The time is September, 1180. Your teacher has asked you to interview Baron Gunther, who recently returned from a crusade. While you listen to him, you take notes. These notes are listed in the box below.

lack of water	ships
intense heat	diseases
long overland journey	injuries
robbers and criminals	Constantinople's wealth
heavenly reward	religious shrines
possible riches	future plans
strong defenses	deserted countryside
peasants	winter camp
Muslims	

Organize these notes into a written report about the crusader's experiences. Write your report on the lines below in complete sentences. Include all of the information that is given in the notes.

_____

_____

_____

_____

_____

_____

_____

_____

_____

_____

_____

_____

_____

_____

_____

WORKING WITH DIAGRAMS

Cathedrals were built in important trading centers. Government functions, such as weddings, funerals, coronations, and assemblies were held within cathedral walls. People traveled to cathedrals to seek help or pray for a cure from disease. The size and beauty of cathedrals were intended to show God the support of the people for the work of the Church.

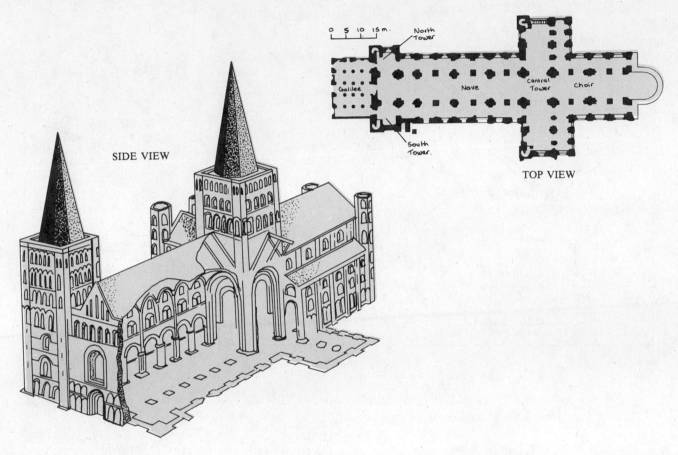

SIDE VIEW

TOP VIEW

Use the diagrams above to help you answer the following questions.

1. If you were a young person from the country making a pilgrimage to this cathedral, what first impression might you have about its size?

    _____

    _____

    _____

    _____

2. What was the shape of its floor plan? _____ What do you think it represented?

    _____

3. How long is this cathedral? _____ How wide: _____

WORKING WITH MAPS

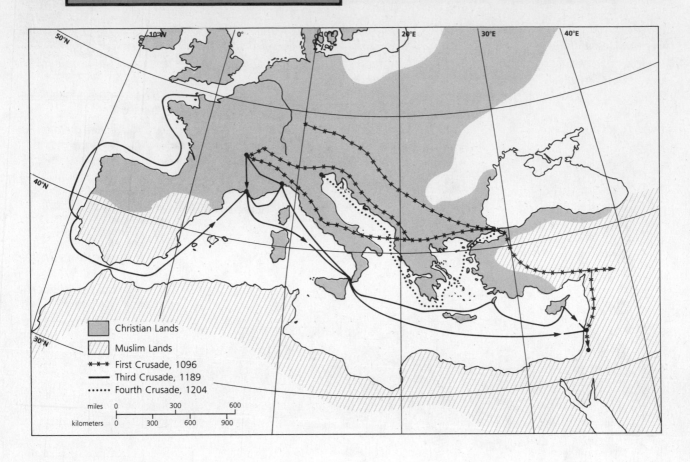

A. On the map above, label the following: *Mediterranean Sea, Adriatic Sea, Aegean Sea, Black Sea, Atlantic Ocean, Palestine, Italy, Asia Minor, Holy Roman Empire, Spain, France, England.*

B. Fill in the blanks below with the names of the cities described in the statements. Label the cities on the map.

_____   1.   city from which the Children's Crusade sailed

_____   2.   capital of the Byzantine Empire

_____   3.   Adriatic port where Fourth Crusade began

_____   4.   city that is the center of the Holy Land

_____   5.   last Christian stronghold in Palestine

Rise of Trade and Towns

FOCUS ON IDEAS

Fill in the blanks to form a summary of Chapter 25. You will find some of the proper terms listed below. For other words, you may need to use your textbook.

artisans	cleanliness	feudalism	North
burgs	cloth	kings	overland
business	crowded	lords	plague
charters	East	metal	products

During the eleventh and twelfth centuries, Venice and Flanders became important centers in the

trade between Europe and the _____. Venetian traders became

full-time merchants and began to develop an effective _____ system. Flemish mer-

chants _____. They made it into

_____ and then shipped the finished product back to England.

Merchants traveled _____ routes and traded their goods at _____.

They later formed permanent settlements that developed into towns known as _____.

As the towns grew without thought to future planning, _____ conditions led to

unhealthy places to live. A _____, believed to have been started by diseased rats on

trading ships from the East, swept through Europe killing millions of people.

During the 1400s, merchants, _____, and bankers became more important than they

had been in the past. They soon controlled the_____ and trade of towns. Townspeople

also demanded and received _____ from feudal lords in order to run their own affairs.

Organizations known as guilds _____.

The growing prosperity of towns led to the decline of_____. As townspeople grew

richer, they began to set fashions and _____.

They turned away from feudal _____ and began to look to _____ to pro-

vide leadership.

USING VOCABULARY

On the left is a list of clues to the coded words in the middle. To decode the words, substitute letters of the alphabet for the letters in each set. Use each clue and its code to spell the answer. For example, P H U F K D Q W spells merchant.

A =__ B =__ C =__ D =__ E =__ F =__ G =__ H =__ I =__ J =__ K =__ L =__ M =__ N =__

O =__ P =__ Q =__ R =__ S =__ T =__ U =__ V =__ W =__ X =__ Y =__ Z =__

Clue	Code	Answer
1. a person who worked under a master for a daily wage	M R X U Q H B P D Q	_____
2. towns that developed from merchant settlements	E X U J V	_____
3. documents that permitted townspeople to control their own affairs	F K D U W H U V	_____
4. instrument used for public punishment	V W R F N V	_____
5. an expert in a trade	P D V W H U	_____
6. rich merchants of the Middle Ages	E X U J K H U V	_____
7. northern Italian political group opposed to the nobles and bishops	F R P P X Q H	_____
8. special gatherings for trading purposes along main highways	I D L U V	_____
9. a trainee in a trade	D S S U H Q W L F H	_____
10. items for sale	Z D U H V	_____
11. cloth woven with a raised design	E U R F D G H	_____
12. business groups formed to ensure equal treatment for all members	J X L O G V	_____

Name _____ Date _____ Class _____

BEING CREATIVE: GUILD BADGES

Guilds were formed to insure that their members were treated equally and to guarantee that quality goods were produced. It was not easy to become a member of a guild. It required much training and skill. Badges were often created to symbolize a guild's craft and to show the members' pride in their work.

A.   Identify the kinds of guilds represented by the following sketches.

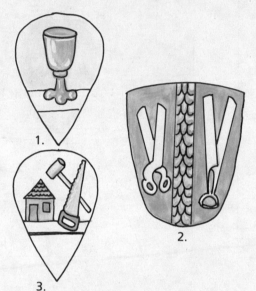

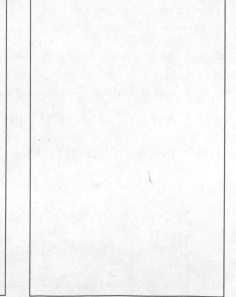

1. _____

2. _____

3. _____

B.   Design a badge of arms for the following occupations if they were to form guilds.

1. Computer Programmers   2. Astronauts   3. Your Future Occupation

Name _____ Date _____ Class _____

Maps can help us compare the changes that cities and countries undergo. The maps below show the changes that took place in Lincoln, England, over a 200-year period.

Map A   **Map B**

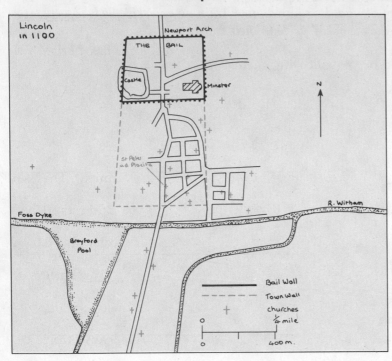

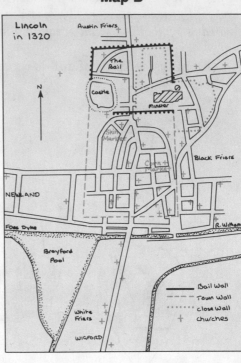

Use the two maps to answer the following questions.

1. What has happened to show growth of this city? _____

_____

2. Did the castle area change very much from Map A to Map B? _____

Why do you think this did or did not change? _____

_____

3. Why are there so many churches on each map? _____

_____

4. List two types of travel into the city from Map B. _____

5. Name two markets on Map B. _____

Why might they not appear on Map A? _____

6. Which group of people probably controlled the city in Map B? (Check Chapter 26 in the *Human*

Heritage text for ideas.) _____

_____

Rise of Monarchies

FOCUS ON IDEAS

Fill in the blanks to form a summary of Chapter 27. You will find some of the proper terms listed below. For other words, you may need to use your textbook.

Capetian	demands	jury	Paris
Charles	Eleanor	limits	Parliament
cities	Ferdinand	longbow	peasants
councils	Isabella	Orleans	taxation

In France, kings of the _____ dynasty strengthened the central government. They set up a national _____, formed an efficient system of _____, and established _____. French monarchs also made _____ the center of government, and granted many _____ charters of freedom.

In England, William the Conqueror introduced Norman customs and based new taxes on _____ figures from the *Domesday Book*. Henry II made the king's law supreme in the land and developed a system of trial by _____. However, King John was forced to accept _____. Later, Edward I set up _____ to advise him and help him make laws.

In the Hundred Years' War, naval successes and a new steel-tipped arrow used with the _____ gave the English the first and greatest victories. However, the French King _____ listened to a young French peasant girl named Joan of Arc who soon _____. Results of the war strengthened the importance of _____ in both countries. Peasants knew they were needed and made _____.

Monarchs were important in Germany and Spain. The _____ family ruled the Holy Roman Empire. But the German territories _____. King Ferdinand and Queen _____ made Spain a Catholic country.

USING VOCABULARY

Chapter 27

The alphabetical list contains the letters for spelling the words that complete the statements below. Complete the statements with the proper word, and cross out the letters used to spell the answers. When all of the statements have been completed, all letters in the alphabetical list will have been used.

A A A A A B C C C C C D D D D D E E E E E E E G G G G H
H I I I I I I I I J J J L L L M N N N N N N N O O O O O P P R
R R R R R R R R S S S S T T T T T U U U U U W Y Y

1. Countries governed by one ruler are called _____.

2. Traveling judges in England were called _____ _____.

3. What word refers to the European mainland? _____

4. The Magna Carta gave freemen accused of crimes the right to a trial by their

   _____, or equals.

5. Henry II of England used the_____ _____, or a group of people

   who presented the names of suspected criminals to traveling judges.

6. A weapon invented during the Hundred Years' War that used steel-tipped arrows was called the

   _____.

7. The group of people who decide whether a person accused of a crime is innocent or guilty is

   called a(n) _____ _____.

8. The German princes met in an assembly called a _____ to elect an emperor of the

   Holy Roman Empire.

9. Royal officials of Spain who governed the towns and set up special law courts were named

   _____.

10. What is the French word for the eldest son of the king?_____

NEWS STORY

Imagine that you are living in France during the Hundred Years' War. Below is a paragraph as it might have appeared in a Paris newspaper in 1429. Read the paragraph and write an additional paragraph of your own beneath it. Use information about Joan of Arc to finish your news story.

Travelers from the countryside report that English soldiers are besieging the city of Orleans. News of the English attack has led to widespread panic. Thousands are fleeing their homes and heading for safe villages and towns.

However, there is a hope for France. _____

_____

_____

_____

_____

_____

_____

_____

_____

_____

_____

SENTENCE BUILDING

Use the word list below to write two sentences on the lines provided. The sentences may include words not found in the list. However, each word in the list should be used.

| Magna Carta | King John | nobles | law | refused |
| taxes | obey | freeman | right | Runnymede |

Sentence 1. _____

_____

Sentence 2. _____

_____

Name _____ Date _____ Class _____

Use your map skills to do the exercise. You may use your textbook to find some of the answers.

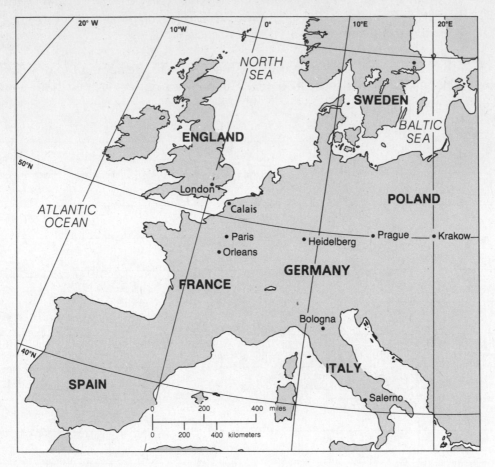

A. 1. Name the city located at: 49° N 2° E   _____

41° N 15° E   _____

2. What are the coordinates for: London?   _____

Heidelberg?   _____

3. About how far is: London from Paris?   _____
miles   kilometers

Calais from Salerno?   _____
miles   kilometers

4. If you are traveling from Bologna to Prague, in which   _____
direction are you going?

B. Fill in the blanks with the names of the cities described in the statements.

_____   the city in which Joan of Arc led an attack
against the English army

_____   last French city held by the English at the end of
the Hundred Years' War

Geography and History

TRADING CONNECTS PEOPLE

People go through major changes because of trading and transportation. Imagine you are completing a ship captain's log on a trading vessel. Fill in the missing information on the log below using the text map on page 400.

DATE	CARGO	DEPARTURE PORT	DESTINATION	PROBLEMS
May 1300				

DATE	CARGO	DEPARTURE PORT	DESTINATION	PROBLEMS
June 1300				

DATE	CARGO	DEPARTURE PORT	DESTINATION	PROBLEMS
late June 1300				

DATE	CARGO	DEPARTURE PORT	DESTINATION	PROBLEMS
late July 1300				

DATE	CARGO	DEPARTURE PORT	DESTINATION	PROBLEMS
September 1300				

Put yourself in the place of the ship's captain. Will you continue trading or do you think there are too many problems? Explain.

_____

_____

UNIT 8 AROUND THE WORLD

FEUDAL JAPAN

A. *Fill in the blanks below with the correct term or name. Use textbook pages 426–427 to help you complete the page.*

1. _____ armed warriors; held in high respect

2. _____ head of Japan's military government

3. _____ an honor code called "the way of the warrior"

4. _____ built to encourage samurai and others to meditate

5. _____ local landlords of feudal Japan

6. _____ symbols of their station worn at the sides of the samurai

B. *Read the following sentences and decide which are relevant to the topic of the life of a samurai. Write* Yes *in the blank beside each statement that contains relevant information on this topic. Write* No *if the statement contains irrelevant information.*

_____ 1. All classes of society respect the samurai's position.

_____ 2. Samurai are trained in the ritual of pouring tea.

_____ 3. Many ancient Japanese people were talented musicians.

_____ 4. Ancient Japanese respected people having good manners and courtesy.

_____ 5. The ancient Japanese cultivated, or grew, rice.

Write a summary statement that supports the following question: "What geographic factors helped the Japanese military sustain their power over the people?"

_____

_____

_____

_____

The Renaissance

FOCUS ON IDEAS

In the summary of Chapter 28, the topic of each paragraph is given. In the first paragraph, fill in the blanks by choosing the proper term from the words listed below. Then write a second paragraph to complete your chapter summary.

Alexander VI	El Escorial	humanist	printing press
artists	Elizabeth I	mechanical digger	religion
church	Erasmus	Medici	Rome
classical	Francis I	Michelangelo	Savonarola
Don Quixote	Hubert Van Eyck	plays	telegraph system

Beginning of the Renaissance in Italy

1. Around 1300, a new interest in _____ writings led to a new age called the Renaissance. People were less concerned about _____ and more interested in the wonders of the world around them. The Renaissance began in Italy, where wealthy merchants supported the work of _____ and scholars. Florence, ruled by the _____ family, became the first center of the Italian Renaissance. Later the movement spread to the cities of _____ and Venice.

Renaissance in Other European Lands

2. _____

_____

_____

_____

_____

_____

_____

_____

USING VOCABULARY

Fill in the missing letters of each word below based on the clues provided.

official ruler of Venice	d _ g _
scholars who believed in the importance of people	h u _ a n _ s t _
word describing the writings of the ancient Greeks and Romans	c l a _ s i _ a _
author of a play	p _ a y _ r i _ _ t
way of painting used to show objects as they appear at different distances	_ e r _ p e c _ i v e
open area in the front and on the sides of a stage	p _ t
French castles designed by Italian Renaissance architects	c _ a _ e a _ x
central square of an Italian Renaissance city	_ i a _ z _
a device to print books that used moveable, carved letters to form words	_ _ i n _ i n _ _ r e _ _

THINKING LOGICALLY

The word logic means a way of thinking in which the thinker seeks truth and accuracy. This activity involves logical thinking about the Renaissance. Read the names or terms listed below. For each name or term, underline the lettered word following that is an example of it.

1. coastal trading city
   - A. Florence
   - B. Venice
   - C. Paris
   - D. Rome

2. Renaissance Pope
   - A. Gregory VII
   - B. Alexander VI
   - C. rebuilt Rome
   - D. led the Catholic Church

3. Renaissance scientists
   - A. painted for the wealthy
   - B. wrote plays
   - C. Petrarch and Durer
   - D. Galileo and Vesalius

4. Italian Renaissance achievements
   - A. Savonarola
   - B. printing press
   - C. Medici
   - D. art and literature

5. English playwright
   - A. William Shakespeare
   - B. Globe Theater
   - C. Erasmus
   - D. musical instruments

BEING CREATIVE: WANT AD FOR A RENAISSANCE ARTIST

A. *Artists were very important in Renaissance life. Each city-state wanted to hire the best artists. Write a want ad for a Renaissance artist as it might appear in a newspaper or magazine.*

Job Description:

Qualifications:

Salary:

B. *What particular Renaissance artist did you have in mind when you wrote your want ad?*

_____   _____
         Name   Country

C. *Do you think the accomplishments of Renaissance artists are still important to artists today? Explain your*

answer. _____

_____

_____

_____

_____

_____

WORKING WITH DIAGRAMS

The Globe Theater was an open-air public playhouse located in the suburbs of London. Most of William Shake-speare's plays were performed there. Read the following description and study the diagram of the Globe Theater. Then, complete the activity that follows.

Many of the spectators stood in the open yard near the stage (1). Covered seating was available for those who could pay the higher price (2). Different stages were used to portray the action. If an outdoor scene was required, the actors appeared on the platform (3). Indoor scenes were played on a curtained inner stage (4). A second-story stage was used for balcony scenes or scenes in heaven (5). Before each performance, trumpets were sounded from the tower (6).

Use the description above and the diagram numbers to indicate on which stage these four scenes from Shake-speare's play Julius Caesar took place.

1. Act I   Scene 1: Rome. A street   _____

2. Act II   Scene 1: Rome. Brutus' garden corner   _____

3. Act II   Scene 2: Rome. Caesar's house   _____

4. Act III   Scene 1: Rome. Before the Capitol   _____

The Reformation

FOCUS ON IDEAS

In the summary of Chapter 29, the topic of each paragraph is given. In the first and second paragraphs, fill in the blank by choosing the proper terms from the words listed below. On the lines provided, write a short paragraph about the Protestant–Catholic rivalry in sixteenth-century Europe.

allow	Henry VIII	Latin	Reformed
Armada	Jesuits	Martin Luther	Seminary
Elizabeth I	John Calvin	Philip II	Spanish
Francis I	Mary	reformation	Trent

Religious Reform in Europe

1. In the 1500s, a religious _____ swept through Europe. The ideas of a German monk named _____ _____ led to the rise of Protestantism. People in northern Europe formed Lutheran and _____ churches. Catholic reformers, such as the _____, worked to improve their church. Between 1545 and 1563, the Council of _____ reformed many church practices.

Reformation in England

2. The Reformation in England began as a quarrel between King _____ and the Pope. Queen _____ tried to force England to return to the Catholic Church. Finally _____ decided that the English Church should be Protestant with some Catholic features. In 1588, the English defeated the Spanish _____ and saved northern Europe for Protestantism.

Protestant-Catholic Rivalry in Europe

3. _____

_____

_____

USING VOCABULARY

Chapter 29

The scrambled words at the beginning of each sentence contain the letters for the two terms needed. Cross off, in order, the letters necessary for the first definition and the term for the second definition will be left.

H E M I R N I S E T T E I R C S

1. Remove a person whose beliefs differ from the accepted beliefs of the Church, or

   _____, and leave _____, or Protestant church leaders.

S T E M H I N E S A R E Y S

2. Remove statements of beliefs, or _____, and leave _____, a school to train priests or ministers.

I R E N F O D U R M L G E A T N I O C N E S

3. Remove documents that freed their owners from punishment for their sins, or

   _____, and leave _____, a change in the teachings and practices of Christianity.

A G A R L L M E A D O N A S

4. Remove a large group of warships, or _____, and leave _____, heavy ships with square-rigged sails and long, raised decks.

SKILL POWER: CRITICAL THINKING

DRAWING CONCLUSIONS

Understanding ideas that are not stated directly requires you to think carefully about what might be the meaning behind the words written or spoken. Place a check in the space provided for each statement that gives evidence to the stated conclusion. Use textbook pages 449–458 to help you complete the page.

A. Martin Luther knew that he would be in trouble if he opposed the Church.

____ As a monk, Luther followed the Church's teachings.

____ He wondered how God would judge his actions.

____ Luther posted his 95 theses in the night.

B. Some Church followers believed improvement had to come from within.

____ Jesuits helped people to strengthen their faith as well as do good deeds.

____ The Council of Trent ended the sale of indulgences.

____ Jesuits worked to bring people back to the Church.

C. *Write a conclusion for the given facts.*

By the middle 1500s, the ruler and people of each country were expected to belong to the same church. There was persecution of people who refused to attend the church they were told to go to. Long and bitter wars were waged over the question of freedom of worship.

_____

_____

Name _____ Date _____ Class _____

IDENTIFYING THE SPEAKER

During the Reformation many religious leaders expressed their ideas. Below are quotations that reflect the thinking of some of these leaders. Read the speakers' quotations and answer the questions on the line provided.

<u>Martin Luther:</u>   "The Church is wrong for selling indulgences. People will get the idea that they can get to heaven with a ticket bought on Earth. Have faith in Jesus alone."

<u>Henry VIII:</u>   "My land and my people are more important than loyalty to the Pope. The safety of England depends upon my having a son. If necessary, I shall become head of the English Church."

<u>Pope Leo X:</u>   "Luther, I excommunicate you from the Church of Christ!"

<u>Ignatius of Loyola:</u>   "Our choice is simple. We will defend the Church against the Protestants by using reason and good deeds."

1. Which speaker believed that pardons for sin could not be bought?

_____

2. Which speaker placed political duties above religious loyalties?

_____

3. Which speaker took definite action against his foe?

_____

4. Which speaker faced the possibility of trial and punishment for his ideas?

_____

5. Which speaker married Anne Boleyn?

_____

6. Which speaker debated his opponents?

_____

7. Which speaker wanted to reform and defend the Catholic Church?

_____

8. Which speaker was a noble who devoted his life to God?

_____

WORKING WITH MAPS

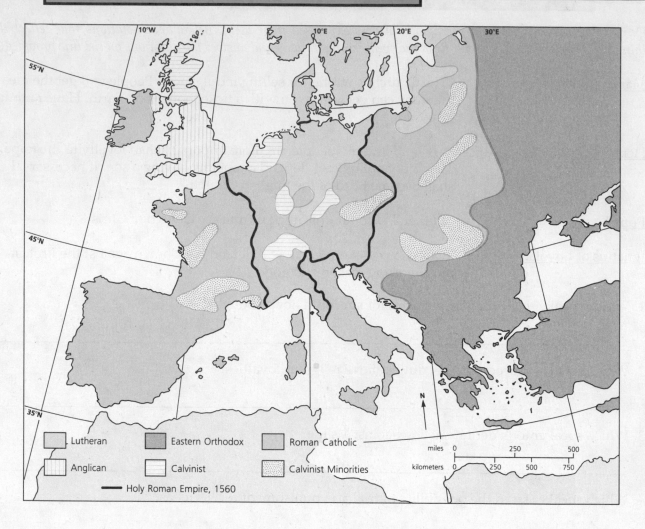

A. On the map, label the following: *Atlantic Ocean, North Sea, Baltic Sea, Mediterranean Sea, Spain, France, Portugal, Low Countries, Switzerland, Italy, Germany, Bohemia, England, Scotland, Ireland, Norway, Sweden, Denmark, Poland, Hungary, and Rus states.*

B. *Identify the cities described below and place the number for each city on the map.*

1. _____ where Luther posted his 95 theses on the castle church door

2. _____ city where a treaty was signed allowing both Roman Catholic and Lutheran churches in Germany

3. _____ town where Roman Catholic leadership discussed church reforms

4. _____ site of St. Peter's Church

5. _____ home of the most powerful Reformed church group

The Age of Discovery

Chapter 30

FOCUS ON IDEAS

In the summary of Chapter 30, the topic of each paragraph is given. In the first paragraph, fill in the blanks by choosing the proper term from the words listed below. Then write a second paragraph to complete your chapter summary.

Africa	France	navigators	rigs
claims	instruments	northeast	safe
direct	Middle East	northwest	Sweden
Far East	Native Americans	ports	

Voyages of Discovery Begin

1. Because of the high cost of goods, European nations began to look for a(n) _____ sea

route to India and the _____ _____. The development of better maps,

ships, and _____ for sailing helped the Europeans in their voyages of discovery. Prince

Henry of Portugal started the first European school for _____. Between 1497 and 1499,

the Portuguese explorer Vasco da Gama sailed from Portugal around _____ to India

and back again.

Portugal and Spain Compete

2. _____

_____

_____

_____

_____

_____

Exploration of the Americas by England, France, and the Netherlands

3. _____

_____

_____

_____

ENLARGING YOUR UNDERSTANDING

Read the following paragraphs. On the lines provided, write the unstated main idea that the writer is emphasizing.

1. Driven by desires for new trade routes, riches, and knowledge about the world, the Portuguese were leaders in exploring areas beyond the Mediterranean Sea. Prince Henry established the first European navigator's school. Those skilled in sea travel became the teachers. They created better charts and improved the navigational instruments. At the same time, Prince Henry was also involved in developing faster and better ships. Explorers who set out to explore the west coast of Africa received encouragement from Prince Henry.

   _____

   _____

   _____

   _____

   _____

   _____

   _____

2. With a strong belief in his own ideas, navigator Christopher Columbus tried to convince different rulers that he could reach India by sailing west. Finally, Queen Isabella of Spain agreed to finance his voyage. Three small ships were provided and Columbus began with a crew of about 90 sailors to sail westward. As the trip progressed, the crews did not share Columbus's dream and they threatened mutiny. Columbus promised they would sight land within three days and the threat was diminished. On the second day, land was sighted. Columbus landed the next day on San Salvador. This was the first of four trips that Columbus made to this new place he had found.

   _____

   _____

   _____

   _____

   _____

   _____

USING VOCABULARY

Chapter 30

Six words are listed for you to define. Use the four given definitions to help you find the four missing vocabulary words. Using the word puzzle below, find the ten words in Column A in the box of letters below. Some words appear horizontally, some vertically, and others diagonally.

```
K  S  C  U  R  V  Y  A  T  C  M  B  A
C  Y  L  O  Y  N  L  N  E  O  U  U  S
H  S  J  E  M  E  T  R  A  N  T  L  T
C  M  E  O  V  P  K  M  S  V  I  L  R
D  E  M  A  R  C  A  T  I  O  N  I  O
O  R  R  T  D  N  O  S  N  Y  Y  O  L
N  A  U  S  M  O  R  O  S  B  X  N  A
C  W  L  E  T  L  G  O  E  M  A  E  B
C  O  N  Q  U  I  S  T  A  D  O  R  E
```

	A	B
	Word	**Definition**
1.	mutiny	_____
2.	conquistadore	_____
3.	scurvy	_____
4.	caravel	_____
5.	_____	a dividing line
6.	_____	gold and silver for making coins
7.	sea dog	_____
8.	_____	instrument with a needle that always points north
9.	_____	groups of ships traveling together
10.	astrolabe	_____

WORKING WITH MAPS

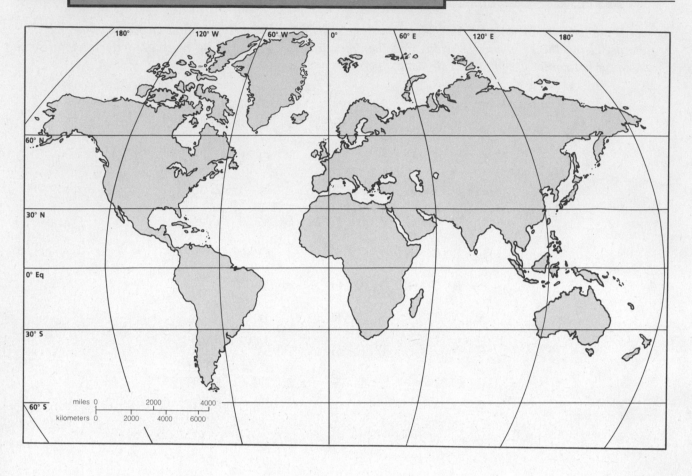

A. On the map above, label the following: North America, South America, Africa, Asia, Europe, Australia. Also label: Pacific Ocean, Atlantic Ocean, Indian Ocean, Cape of Good Hope, Strait of Magellan. Circle the Philippine Islands.

B. Fill in each blank below with the name of the explorer described. Put the number and an X on the map in the area where he explored.

_____ 1. rounded the tip of Africa

_____ 2. reached India by sea around Africa

_____ 3. explored the coasts of Newfoundland and Nova Scotia

_____ 4. explored the waters of the Bahamas, Cuba, and Hispaniola

_____ 5. sailed around tip of South America

_____ 6. sailed to Mexico

_____ 7. explored Peru

_____ 8. sailed on river near present-day Albany, New York

_____ 9. first European to cross the Isthmus of Panama

Geography and History

BEGINNING OF MODERN TIMES

Use the map of Renaissance Italy to answer the questions about trade and travel below.

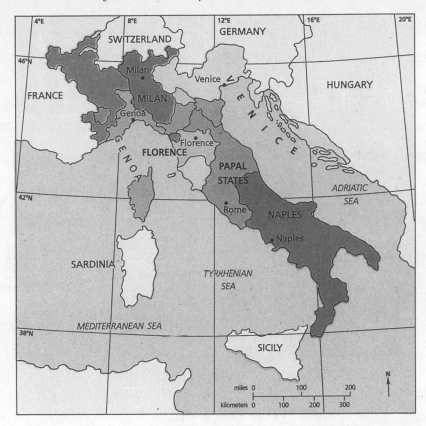

1. A traveler going from Naples to Rome would have to travel about _____ miles, in

   the_____ direction.

2. The Pope leaving Rome and traveling to Florence and Milan, would travel a total of _____

   miles, in the _____ direction.

3. If the Pope sent messengers to both Venice and Genoa at the same time, which messenger would

   most likely return first? _____ About how many miles had

   that messenger traveled? _____

4. Which trade route would seem likely to earn the most money: Milan to Genoa, or Naples to Flo-

   rence? _____ Why? _____

   _____

UNIT 9 AROUND THE WORLD

THE SWAHILI CULTURE

Complete the following questions by writing the answers on the blanks below. Use textbook pages 480–481 to help you complete the page.

A. 1. What does the term "Swahili" mean? _____

2. What evidence supports the idea that East African harbor towns and China traded a wide

variety of goods? _____

_____

3. What are the present-day countries which make up the Swahili culture? _____

_____

4. Why was the blending of cultures of African peoples so vital to Eastern Africa? _____

_____

5. What religion was introduced by Arab traders? _____

6. What contributions did the Arabs make to the trade of Swahili merchants? _____

_____

B. *Imagine you are sharing information about the Swahili culture on the Internet. Design a Web site to lead others to inquire about how many influences from the past affect Swahili culture today. Include: transportation, trading goods, and artifacts found.*

Expansion Into the Americas

FOCUS ON IDEAS

In the summary of Chapter 31, the topic of each paragraph is given. In the first paragraph, fill in the blanks by choosing the proper term from the words listed below. Then write a second and third paragraph to complete your chapter summary.

Atlantic	gold	Pacific	representative
Brazil	largest	Pilgrims	rivals
colonial	Native Americans	plantations	thirteen

The Portuguese and Spanish Empires

1. The Portuguese settled _____, where they owned large _____ worked

by enslaved Africans. The Spanish conquered _____ _____ civilizations

in Mexico and Peru. They established the _____ empire in the Americas. When the

Spanish Armada was defeated in 1588, Spain lost its power in the _____ Ocean.

English Colonies in North America

2. _____

_____

_____

_____

_____

French Settlements in the Americas

3. _____

_____

_____

_____

_____

USING VOCABULARY

Chapter 31

Unscramble the letters in the first column to spell out the term being described in the second column. Write the unscrambled word in the appropriate spaces in the third column. Then, to find the word puzzler, write the circled letters from the third column in order from top to bottom in the spaces provided at the end of the activity.

1. calomsuc — Spice Islands — Ⓞ _ _ _ _ _ _ _

2. sntrdabnieae — fortune hunters — _ Ⓞ _ _ _ _ _ _ _ _

3. cyiaovsreltie — Spanish districts in the New World — _ _ _ _ _ Ⓞ _ _ _ _ _

4. Ibaacen fo dtera — ability of a country to sell as much as it buys — _ _ _ _ _ _ _ _ Ⓞ
_ _ _ _ _

5. Issmayu — places for the mentally ill — _ _ _ Ⓞ _ _

6. lereocs — people of Spanish descent born in the Americas — _ _ _ Ⓞ _ _

7. abzwoidolr — red wood used to make dyes — _ _ _ _ _ Ⓞ _ _

8. pnsctiicaea — 15 territorial strips into which colonial Brazil was divided — _ _ _ _ _ _ _ Ⓞ _

9. rsgbsuese — Virginia's first lawmaking representatives — _ Ⓞ _ _ _ _ _ _

10. Izoinceo — to build permanent settlements — Ⓞ _ _ _ _ _ _

11. eoiyvrc — ruler of a Spanish territory in the Americas — _ _ _ _ _ Ⓞ _

12. szeotmsi — people of mixed European and Native American ancestry — Ⓞ _ _ _ _ _ _

13. saepeinnsurl — Spaniards born in Spain — Ⓞ _ _ _ _ _ _ _ _ _ _

14. eturindedn sstvsrena — people who agreed to work 4-7 years in return for passage to the Americas — _ _ _ _ _ _ _ _
_ _ _ _ Ⓞ _

15. aclgnina — England's official church name — _ _ _ _ _ Ⓞ _ _

16. patsseirast — people looking for religious freedom in the Americas — _ _ _ _ _ _ Ⓞ _ _

??Word Puzzler?? — _ _ _ _ _ _ _ _

_ _ _ _ _ _

LETTER TO THE EDITOR

Some colonists in the Americas wanted to encourage more people to leave Europe and come to their colonies. Imagine that you are such a colonist in one of the following places: Brazil, Mexico, Jamestown, or Quebec. Write a letter to a newspaper in the home country describing life in the Americas. Before you write, decide on what approach you want to take. Do you want to be realistic and write about the advantages and disadvantages of colonial life, or do you want to attract people with stories of wealth? Also, consider what should be general health, ages, and skills of Europeans you want to bring to the Americas.

September 23, 1700

Dear Editor:

_____

_____

_____

_____

_____

_____

_____

_____

_____

_____

_____

_____

Sincerely,

_____

Name _____ Date _____ Class _____

A. *On the map, label the following: North America, South America, New Spain, Brazil, Peru, West Indies, Louisiana, Florida, Hudson Bay, Mississippi River, Atlantic Ocean, Pacific Ocean.*

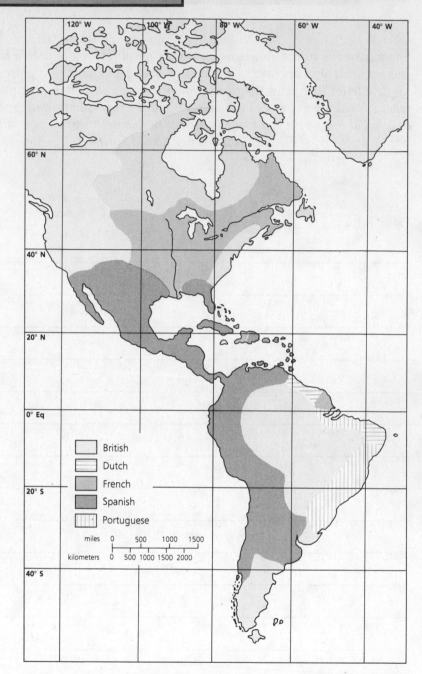

British

Dutch

French

Spanish

Portuguese

miles   0   500   1000   1500

kilometers   0   500 1000 1500 2000

B. *Fill in the blanks below with the names of the colonies described in the statements. Place the numbers on the map to indicate the location of the colonies.*

_____   1. first permanent English colony in North America

_____   2. colony founded by Pilgrims

_____   3. colony founded by the Dutch

_____   4. Spanish colony also called New Castile

_____   5. Spanish colony today called Mexico

_____   6. first permanent French colony in the Americas

Political Revolutions

Chapter
32

FOCUS ON IDEAS

In the summary of Chapter 32, the topic of each paragraph is given. In the first paragraph, fill in the blanks by choosing the proper term from the words listed below. Then write a second paragraph to complete your chapter summary.

Charles I	"Glorious	limited	Puritans
Declaration of	Revolution"	monarchy	schools
Independence	independent	peace	Third Estate
Declaration of	James II	conference	
Rights			

Growth of Self-Government

1. During the seventeenth century, England underwent a political_____. Disagreements between King _____ and Parliament led to a(n) _____

_____. In 1649, the _____ overthrew the king and executed him. In 1660,

Parliament _____ the monarchy. After the _____ _____ of

1688, it limited the king's powers and passed the _____. The English Revolution later influenced others. In 1776, disagreements between England and the American

colonies led to a war that made the colonies a(n) _____ nation. In 1789, the United

States adopted a(n) _____ which established a democratic government.

Achievements of the French Revolution

2. _____

_____

_____

_____

_____

_____

_____

_____

USING VOCABULARY ══════════════════════════ **Chapter 32**

From the definitions given, find the proper term to fill in the missing letters of each line of Parts A, B, and C. Then, using the numbered letters from each term, fill in the missing letters for the mystery words for A, B, and C, and write their definitions on the lines provided.

A.

— — — — — — —
    4   7 7

refuse to buy

— — — — — —   — — —
  8 3 2 4 7   7 5

tax paid to government, not included in price of goods

— — — — — —   — — — — — —
  3 2 10   6   9 8

relations with other countries

— — — — — — — — — —
5 12 2 6   1 2 6 7 11

formal changes

— — — — — — — — — — — —
1 2 3 4 5 6 7 8 9 10 11 12

_____

_____

_____

B.

— — — — — — — — — —
21 6 14 2 4 16   21   4

educated French; means philosophers

— — — — — — — — — —
15 13 19 9 10 13 14   14 18

rule by the army, rather than by law

— — — — — — — —
  8 6 14 14 2 7 10 12

machine designed to execute a human by cutting off the head

— — — — - — — — — — —
4 18 17 4   20 8 14 11 5 7

French city worker

— — — — — — —
15 11 12 16   2 14 22

sole right on a product or service

— — — — — — — — —
19   2 14 8 9 10 11 3

an attempt to overthrow or change the government

— — — — — — — — — — — — — —
  2 3 4 5 6 7 8 9 10 11 12 13 14

— — — — — — — —
15 16 17 18 19 20 21 22

_____

_____

_____

(continued)

USING VOCABULARY, cont.

C.

$\overline{5}\ \overline{14}\quad \overline{14}\ \overline{17}\ \overline{11}$ idea that government may use only powers given to it by the people

$\overline{15}\ \overline{9}\ \overline{10}\ \overline{13}\ \overline{7}\ \overline{16}\quad \overline{13}\ \overline{16}$

$\overline{7}\ \overline{11}\ \overline{3}\ \overline{13}\ \overline{6}\ \overline{5}\ \overline{11}$ to have an act abolished

$\overline{17}\ \overline{18}\ \overline{12}\ \overline{6}\ \overline{16}\ \overline{16}\ \overline{18}$ unjust use of power by a ruler

$\overline{9}\ \overline{4}\ \overline{7}\ \overline{15}\ \overline{11}\ \overline{2}\ \overline{14}\ \overline{8}\ \overline{14}\ \overline{13}$ top level of the French Third Estate

$\overline{2}\ \overline{3}\ \overline{4}\ \overline{5}\ \overline{6}\ \overline{7}$ _____

$\overline{8}\ \overline{9}\ \overline{10}\ \overline{11}\ \overline{12}\ \overline{13}\ \overline{14}\ \overline{15}\ \overline{16}\ \overline{17}\ \overline{18}$ _____

SKILL POWER: TECHNOLOGY SKILLS

BUILDING A DATABASE

To keep a list, file, or collection of information on a computer is known as creating a database. Identify the terms to use when building a database by filling in the spaces provided. Use the words in the box below. Textbook page 516 will help you complete the page.

A. 1. _____ specific types of information organized for a database

2. _____ to clear out or erase on a computer

3. _____ a collection of facts stored in a file on a computer

4. _____ to make information more current

5. _____ to tell the computer what to do

6. _____ action for a computer to gather information to display on the screen

fields	update	retrieve
delete	command	electronic database

B. List at least two ways to command your computer to organize information in a database.

_____

_____

WORKING WITH CHARTS

The chart below compares the sizes and privileges of the major classes of French society before the French Revolution. Study the chart, then answer the questions that follow.

Estate	Group(s)	Size (Percentage of total population)	Voting Rights within the Estates General	Taxes paid	Property owned
I	Clergy	1%	one vote	none	10%
II	Nobility	2%	one vote	none	20%
III	Bourgeoisie & Peasants	17% & 80%	one vote	none	70%

1. How many classes did French society have before the French Revolution? _____

_____

2. What two groups made up the Third Estate? _____

3. What percentage of the total population was the Third Estate? _____

How much property did it own? _____

4. What percentage of the total population were the First and Second Estates? _____

How much property did they own? _____

5. Do you think the division of voting rights within the Estates-General was fair? _____

Why? _____

_____

_____

6. Why might the conditions presented in this chart lead to a revolution? _____

_____

_____

_____

Rise of Industry

FOCUS ON IDEAS

In the summary of Chapter 33, the topic of each paragraph is given. In the first paragraph, fill in the blanks by choosing the proper term from the words listed below. Then write a second paragraph to complete your chapter summary.

Agricultural Revolution	manufactured goods	scientific method
Bessemer Process	organizing production	steel
bronze	population	textile
Industrial Revolution	production	transportation

Rise and Development of the Industrial Revolution

1. The Scientific Revolution occurred as scientists began to break away from old ideas and to test

their thinking using the _____ _____. At the same time, changes in farm-

ing led to an _____ _____. Greater production of food meant a healthier,

larger _____. This brought increased demands for many different kinds of

_____ _____. The _____ industry led Great Britain into a

new age called the _____ _____. New _____ were built

near rivers to use water power to run _____ and increase production. The factory sys-

tem included interchangeable parts, automation, and the assembly line—all better ways of

_____ _____. _____ was improved with the invention of

the railroad and the steamboat.

Effects of the Industrial Revolution on Society

2. _____

_____

_____

_____

_____

_____

_____

_____

USING VOCABULARY   **Chapter 33**

Fill in the squares by spelling out the terms given in the clues below.

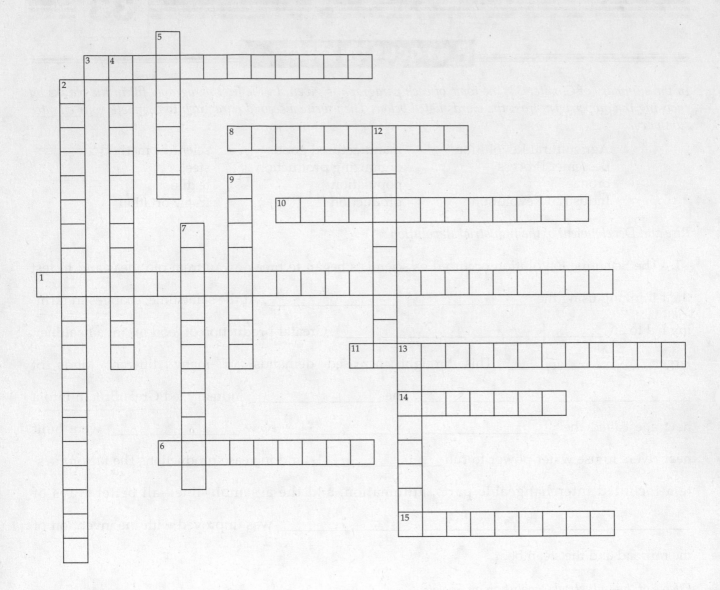

ACROSS

1. engine fueled by gasoline
3. system in which each worker adds a single part to a product until it is completed
6. British method of land division
8. permanent settlers in a different country
10. brought workers and machines together to make goods
11. increased industry
14. road with a surface made of layers of crushed stones
15. cotton-cleaning machine

DOWN

2. system in which the same products all have parts of the same shape and size
4. invention to speed up process of weaving
5. woven cloth
7. workers' associations
9. fuel made by burning wood
12. process in which machines instead of people do much of the labor
13. system in which work is done in homes

Name _____ Date _____ Class _____

BEING CREATIVE: BE AN INVENTOR

As scientists broke away from old ideas, new thoughts and inventions led to great changes in the lives of people. Manufacturing and industry reduced human labor, cities grew rapidly, and the quality of life improved. This activity lets you use your imagination to develop a fresh approach for a common item.

A. *Every student is aware of a school pen and some if its uses. List below how you use a school pen.*

1. _____   5. _____

2. _____   6. _____

3. _____   7. _____

4. _____   8. _____

B. *Imagine how the school pen could be improved upon as a tool for communication. List below a few of your thoughts or ideas for improvement.*

1. _____   5. _____

2. _____   6. _____

3. _____   7. _____

4. _____   8. _____

C. *Draw a sketch to show how your new, improved school pen might look. Label parts to help explain, if necessary.*

Name _____ Date _____ Class _____

A. *The Industrial Revolution brought many changes in people's lives. One result of industrialization was the growth of cities. Use the information in the chart showing the shifting population in English cities to fill in the circle graphs and the bar graph below.*

Population Locations	1781	1801	1851	1891
Percent of English people living in cities of 5,000 or more	15	25	45	68
Percent of English people living in towns and villages	85	75	55	32

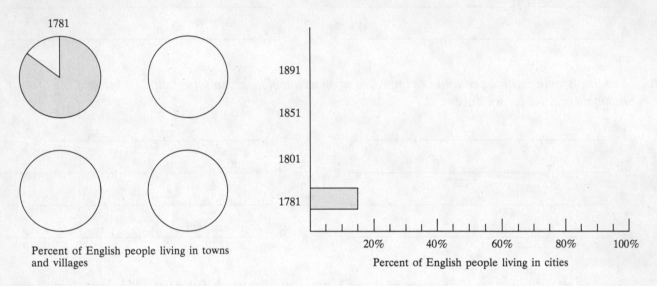

Percent of English people living in towns and villages

Percent of English people living in cities

B. *Study the graphs and answer the following questions.*

1. Between what years did the number of English people living in cities increase by 10 percent?

   _____

2. By what percentage did the number of English people living in towns and villages drop

   between 1781 and 1891? _____

3. What general statement can you make about the effect of the Industrial Revolution on English

   cities? _____

   _____

Geography and History

LOCATING INDUSTRIAL REGIONS

Industrial Revolution.

Use the map below to answer the questions about England's industries at this time.

Industrial England after 1850

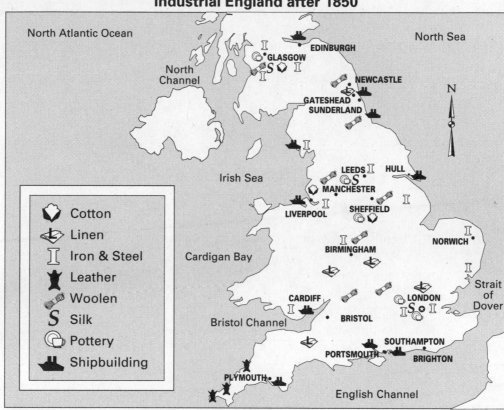

1. Which southern cities were shipbuilding centers? _____

    What was the northernmost shipbuilding city? _____

2. What other industries were most often located in the same area as iron and steel industries?

    _____ Why do you think this happened? _____

    _____

3. What industry was not located near iron and steel production? _____

    Why? _____

4. What industrial area of England offered the most industry? _____

    Why? _____

UNIT 10 AROUND THE WORLD

RUSSIA

You are an expert on Russian culture who has been asked to read a student report about the country and its people. You realize there are several mistakes in the report. Underline the incorrect facts and rewrite the report correctly on the lines below. Use textbook pages 538–539 to help you complete the page.

Russian czars ruled territory east of the Alps and westward to Europe. The heart of the empire always lay west of the Ural Mountains. Development of commerce, transportation, and government control is easy in sprawling lands.

Peter the Great worked hard to westernize Russia. He founded St. Petersburg on the Bering Sea. Catherine the Great impoverished the empire so that by the end of the 1700s, it had reached some 6,000 miles from north to south.

The population was very diverse. People's occupations ranged from hunters on the tundra to farmers in the east. Russian people told proud folktales about their country's industrialization.

Russia was mainly an urban nation, with nearly all of its population working as serfs or living in remote villages.

_____

_____

_____

_____

_____

_____

_____

_____

_____

_____

_____

_____

_____

_____

The Americas

FOCUS ON IDEAS

In the summary of Chapter 34, the topic of each paragraph is given. In the first paragraph, fill in the blanks by choosing the proper term from the words listed below. Then write a second paragraph to complete your chapter summary.

agricultural	democratic	elections	reduced
Canada	doubled	industrial	war

The United States

1. After the United States became independent, _____ political parties developed. Power passed from one president to another through _____ rather than through _____. By 1830, the government of the United States had become one of the most _____ in the world. By 1853, it had more than _____ in size with the addition of such territories as _____, Texas, California, and Oregon. After the _____ _____ of 1861-1865, the United States began to develop into a strong industrial nation.

Latin American Independence

2. _____

    _____

    _____

    _____

    _____

    _____

    _____

    _____

    _____

    _____

Name _____ Date _____ Class _____

A.   Fill in the missing letters of each word below based on the clue provided.

groups with different ideas about govern-   p _ l i _ i c _ l   p a _ t i _ _
ment

rules from year to year without great   s _ a _ l e
changes   g o _ e r _ m _ n t

growth of cities   _ r b _ _ i z _ _ i o n

act of taking over a territory and combining   a _ n e _ a t _ _ _ n
it with an existing country

old houses or commercial buildings made   _ e n _ m e _ _ _ _
into apartments for the lower class

national   f _ _ e r a _

withdrawing from being part of a nation   _ e c e _ i n g

a committee organized to take over a gov-   j u _ t _
ernment

Latin American leader, or strong man   _ a u _ i l _ o

areas containing large numbers of tene-   s _ u _ s
ments

idea that the United States should stretch   m _ _ i _ _ s t
from the Atlantic Ocean to the Pacific   _ e s _ i _ y
Ocean

B.   Write four sentences using at least one of the words or phrases listed above in each. Underline the words
that you use from the above list.

_____

_____

_____

_____

_____

_____

_____

Name _____ Date _____ Class _____

A. *Imagine that you are living in 1850 and that you are heading to the American West in a wagon train with your family. The trip will take three months. You will face muddy roads, violent rivers, and harsh weather. At some point in your trip, you may have to discard some of your belongings. Below is a list of the items in your wagon. Write "yes" beside each item you will need. Write "no" beside each item you will not need.*

_____ wheat seed (2 bushels)   _____ tent

_____ mattress and brass bed   _____ expensive violin

_____ dairy cow   _____ 100 feet of rope

_____ wood logs for fuel   _____ horseshoes and nails

_____ jewelry   _____ trunk containing clothes

_____ 8 oxen and 2 horses   _____ saw and ax

_____ musket and other weapons   _____ cage of 3 chickens

_____ 4 bolts of cloth   _____ sewing machine

_____ steel-blade land plow   _____ books

_____ pots, pans, and silverware   _____ wood-burning cook stove

B. *On the lines below, write briefly about your plans when you reach the end of your journey. Mention the area in which you will settle and its features, the type of work you might do, and how you will use some of the above items in adjusting to a new way of life.*

_____

_____

_____

_____

_____

_____

_____

_____

_____

_____

Name _____ Date _____ Class _____

A. Clocks in different parts of the world do not show the same time because the world is divided into time zones. The map below shows the times in each part of the world when it is 12 o'clock noon at the Prime Meridian (0°).

B. Study the map and answer the questions that follow.

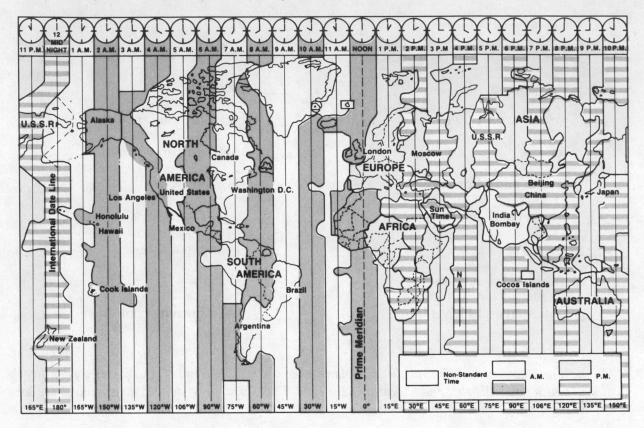

1. Are the time zones based on lines of latitude or lines of longitude? _____

2. When it is noon along the Prime Meridian, what time is it in these cities?

Washington, D.C. _____   Bombay _____

Honolulu _____   Tokyo _____

Beijing _____   London _____

3. If it were 3 P.M. along the Prime Meridian, what time is it in these cities?

Washington, D.C. _____   Bombay _____

Honolulu _____   Tokyo _____

Beijing _____   London _____

Unrest in Europe

FOCUS ON IDEAS

In the summary of Chapter 35, the topic of each paragraph is given. In the first paragraph, fill in the blanks by choosing the proper term from the words listed below. Then write a second and third paragraph to complete your chapter summary.

French Revolution	law code	press	speech
Germany	monarchy	Russia	western

Napoleon

1. Napoleon Bonaparte strengthened the central government of France and set up a single law code for the entire nation. However, he did not allow freedom of speech or the press. The French leader conquered most of western Europe and did much to spread the ideas of the French Revolution. The Allied nations, led by Russia, Austria, Prussia, and England, finally defeated Napoleon at the Battle of Waterloo in 1815.

Reaction, Revolution, and Reform

2. _____

_____

_____

_____

_____

_____

_____

Growth of Nationalism

3. _____

_____

_____

_____

USING VOCABULARY

The scrambled words at the beginning of each sentence contain the letters for the two terms needed. Cross off, in order, the letters necessary for the first definition and the term for the second definition will be left.

C O P M L M E U B I N S C I I S T E M

1. Remove popular vote, or _____, and leave _____, a type of socialism developed by Karl Marx, who believed a workers' revolution would create a society without hunger and poverty.

S C G U E O R R R C H I L L A E D W E A R A R F T H A P O R L I E C Y

2. Remove a tactic used in war in which villages and food supplies are burned, leaving nothing for the enemy to use, or _____-_____ _____, and leave_____ _____, a kind of fighting in which small bands of soldiers behind enemy lines make surprise attacks.

A B B A D L A I N C C E O A F P O W T E E R

3. Remove to give up the throne, or_____, and leave_____, or equal strength among nations.

L I S O B C I A E L R I A S L T S S

4. Remove middle-class believers in political reform based on individual freedoms and rights, or _____, and leave _____, or those who believe the only way to bring about reform is through revolution.

K A P R O I S L E E T A R R I A T E

5. Remove a German title for emperor, or _____, and leave _____, or industrial working class.

S U N I V T R E R S A L I K M A L E S U F E F R A G E

6. Remove to stop work to obtain rights, or _____, and leave _____ _____, or the right of all males to vote.

Name _____ Date _____ Class _____

Imagine that you are a reporter interviewing several nineteenth-century political leaders about their ideas. The leaders are: William Gladstone, a liberal; Giuseppe Garibaldi, a nationalist; and Louis Blanc, a socialist. On the lines provided, write the responses these leaders might give to the following questions.

Question 1.   "Mr. Gladstone, where in Europe are your liberal ideas most popular? What changes have they brought?"

Response: _____

_____

Question 2.   "Mr. Garibaldi, you have been called a nationalist. What does this word mean to you?"

Response: _____

_____

Question 3.   "Mr. Blanc, what kinds of people might choose socialism, and what might be a reason

for this choice?"

Response: _____

_____

SKILL POWER: CRITICAL THINKING

PREDICTING CONSEQUENCES

Intelligent "guessing" is learning the skill of how to identify logical results of decisions or actions. Review the facts given, and look for any patterns that may exist. Then select your own prediction for the final box by placing a check by one of the choices given. Use textbook pages 572–574 to help you complete the page.

EVENTS IN ITALY 1848-1861	RESULTS AND REACTIONS
In 1848, 8 of 9 Italian states were ruled by Austria	People of Italy were unhappy about this state of affairs.
In 1859, France joined Sardinia to defeat Austria.	Lombardy, other Italian state, was united with Sardinia.
Other northern Italian states revolted against Austria in 1860, while in the south, Garibaldi trained followers in guerrilla warfare.	In 1861, northern and southern nationalists groups combined to form a constitutional monarchy.
The Pope, who wanted to keep control over the Papal States, fought against the Italians and lost.	?????????????????????????

Select your prediction: _____   European balance of power was strengthened.

_____   Kingdom of Italy permitted the Pope to rule the Papal States.

_____   Italian unification was complete.

Name _____ Date _____ Class _____

As nationalistic feelings increased, countries began to adopt symbols that they felt represented their best characteristics and qualities. Study the pictures below to help you answer the questions.

1.   What do all of these symbols have in common? _____

_____

2.   What are some human characteristics that the symbols might represent? _____

_____

3.   The figure from Great Britain resembles the statue of Athena, the Greek goddess of wisdom.

Why would a nation select this figure as a symbol? _____

_____

4.   The figure from France is wearing a head covering like the French women did in their revolu-

tions, and her hair is flowing freely. What might this symbolize about the French people? _____

_____

_____

LEADERSHIP AND REVOLUTION

During the world revolutions of the 1800s, many unusually strong leaders emerged. These leaders each accomplished things that had an impact on other people. List these accomplishments for each leader shown below and draw some conclusions about what makes a strong leader.

Napolean Bonaparte

Accomplishments:

_____

_____

_____

_____

_____

_____

Karl Marx

Accomplishments:

_____

_____

_____

_____

_____

_____

Giuseppe Garibaldi

Accomplishments:

_____

_____

_____

_____

_____

_____

Characteristics of a strong ruler:

_____

_____

_____

_____

_____

_____

_____

DIALOGUE AND REPORTING

A. Imagine that you are a student living in Paris in the year 1814. You have an opportunity to interview Napoleon Bonaparte. On the lines provided, write at least four questions you would ask the French leader.

_____

_____

_____

_____

_____

_____

_____

_____

B. You are a news correspondent sent to cover the European revolutions of the mid-1800s. Write a brief news story describing the political situation and the outbreak of revolution in either Germany, Austria, or Italy at this time. Include a headline with your story.

_____

_____

_____

_____

_____

_____

_____

_____

_____

Rise of Imperialism

Chapter 36

In the summary of Chapter 36, the topic of each paragraph is given. In the first paragraph, fill in the blanks by choosing the proper term from the words listed below. Then write a second and third paragraph to complete your chapter summary.

England	marines	Russia
France	missionaries	Spain

Imperialism in Africa

1. European explorers and _____ brought more interests of western Europe to the African interior. By 1900, _____ had expanded its territory and had the largest European empire in Africa. _____ had taken over territory that stretched from Cairo to the southernmost Cape of Good Hope. Only two African nations kept their freedom—Ethiopia and _____.

Imperialism in Asia

2. _____

_____

_____

_____

_____

_____

Attempted Imperialism in Latin America

3. _____

_____

_____

_____

Name _____ Date _____ Class _____

United States Territories

4. _____

_____

_____

Effects of Imperialism

5. _____

_____

_____

USING VOCABULARY   **Chapter 36**

The alphabetical list contains the letters for spelling the words that complete the statements below. Complete the statements with the proper terms and cross out the letters used to spell the answers. When all the statements have been completed, there will be some letters left. Unscramble the letters to form a word that will help you answer Part B on the following page.

A.   A A A A A A B C C C C E E E E E E E E E F I I I I I I I I I I L L L M M M

N N N N O O O O O O O P P P P P R R R R R R R S S S S S S S T T T T T T

T T U U U X Y Y Z

1.   What name is given to the policy practiced in the late 1800s by European powers and the United States to establish colonies and build empires? _____

2.   In Japan, rich and powerful families who controlled many industries were called the

_____.

3.   A country under the control and protection of a larger, stronger nation is called a

_____.

4.   Indian soldiers who served in the British army in the late 1800s were called _____.

5.   Special rights given to a stronger nation by a weaker nation are referred to as

_____.

6.   The right of _____ means that foreigners can only be tried for

suspected wrongdoings by their own court system.

B. Write a paragraph to explain how a nation can increase its power by setting up special rights in a smaller foreign country. What is this called? Use the clue word in your writing. *(The clue word is influence.)*

_____

_____

_____

BACK TO THE PAST BY DIALOGUE

An inference is a conclusion based on various facts. Read the imaginary dialogue between Dr. David Livingstone, a Scottish medical missionary, and the United States reporter, Henry Stanley. Then, decide which of the statements below the dialogue represent a fact, an inference, or neither, due to lack of information. Place "F" for fact, "I" for inference, or "N" for neither in the spaces provided.

Stanley: Dr. Livingstone, I presume?

Livingstone: Yes, and who might you be with the flag of the United States?

Stanley: I am Henry Stanley from New York. My search for you has lasted for over two years. The world believes that you are dead since your interesting letters stopped very quickly without an obvious reason.

Livingstone: My man, Stanley, I have been very busy. I have traveled over great areas of the African interior. Letters were not easy to write when the work increased. Do you know how many of these people need help? There are so many different things to learn and places to explore. Diseases of unknown origin affect these wonderful people. There is much to be done.

Stanley: I know. In my travels looking for you I have been inspired to learn all I can about this great continent. It almost seems an accident that I would find you in this remote village here at Lake Tanganyika. May I spend some time here talking to you? I might just be able to get more involved in the further exploration of this vast land.

_____ 1. Dr. Livingstone was concerned for the people of Africa's interior.

_____ 2. Livingstone was very sick and unable to write.

_____ 3. Stanley was an opportunist who just wanted to make money for himself.

_____ 4. Both Livingstone and Stanley realized that their expeditions would lead to the exploitation of the African people.

_____ 5. Livingstone had given up on his mission to convert Africans to Christianity.

_____ 6. Stanley had looked for over two years for Livingstone.

Name _____ Date _____ Class _____

WORKING WITH MAPS

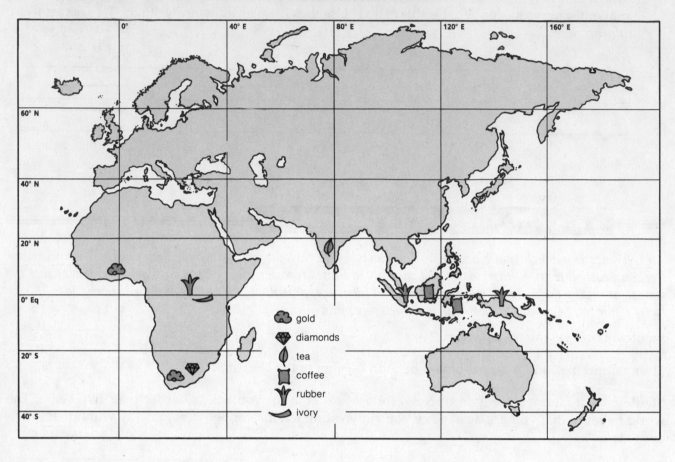

On the map above, label the following: *Atlantic Ocean, Pacific Ocean, Indian Ocean, Great Britain, France, Germany, Belgium, Netherlands, Japan, Russia, Australia. Draw in and label the Suez Canal. Then, fill in the blanks below with the names of areas described in the statements and label them on the map.*

_____

1. area that contained the combined colonies of Cochin-China, Kampuchea, Annam, and Laos

_____

2. British-ruled area where the sepoys revolted

_____

3. area where the British fought the Boers

_____

4. Belgian colony located in central Africa

_____

5. country where the Open Door policy was enforced

_____

6. country that became a British protectorate in 1882

Geography and History

UNIT
11

CHANGING POLITICAL BOUNDARIES

War often changes political boundaries. Some nations lose land. Other countries expand boundaries. Sometimes a new country is formed. Compare the maps on page 564 and 567 of your textbook that show Europe before and after Napoleonic wars.

1. Which country was divided by the Congress of Vienna? _____

   What problems might arise with this kind of governmental arrangement?

   _____

   _____

2. What island country gained land on the mainland of Europe? _____

   What island kingdom gained land on the Italian peninsula? _____

3. What happened to the French Empire as a result of this treaty? _____

   _____

4. How was the size of Switzerland affected by this treaty? _____

5. Describe how the Confederation of the Rhine was affected by this treaty?

   _____

   _____

6. What European countries' boundaries were unchanged by this treaty?

   _____

   Why do you think this was true? _____

   _____

   _____

   _____

   _____

   _____

UNIT 11 AROUND THE WORLD

TIBET

For every event there is a cause. The development and decline of Tibet had many causes. Fill in the blanks below to complete the causes and effects that influenced this country. Use textbook pages 596–597 to help you complete the page.

CAUSE	EFFECT

Tibet is bordered by high mountains and dry plains, with an average _____ of 12,000 feet. It is one of the most _____ regions on earth.

➡️

Tibet's _____ helped protect its independence.

Many Tibetans still live as their _____ did. They load trade goods—salt, cheese, rugs and other items—onto horses or _____ and travel along old caravan routes.

➡️

For much of Tibet's history, _____ have occupied the territory.

Buddhism is said to have been brought to _____ , the capital of Tibet, in the early 600s. Tibet developed into a theocracy. In the early 1900s, almost 500,000 Buddhist _____ lived in Tibet.

➡️

_____ have led the long struggle for freedom since 1906.

Chinese communist troops brutally put down a Tibetan _____ in 1959. More than 100,000 Tibetans _____ into Nepal, Bhutan, and India.

➡️

Today, the current _____ lives in India.

Conflict and Change

Chapter 37

FOCUS ON IDEAS

Five topics are given below for Chapter 37. Write a paragraph about each topic.

World War I

1. _____
   _____
   _____
   _____
   _____

Between Wars

2. _____
   _____
   _____
   _____
   _____

Rise of Communism in Russia

3. _____
   _____
   _____
   _____
   _____

(continued)

FOCUS ON IDEAS, cont.

World War II

4. _____

_____

_____

_____

Making Peace After World War II

5. _____

_____

_____

_____

USING VOCABULARY   **Chapter 37**

On the left is a list of clues to the coded words in the middle. To decode the words, substitute letters of the alphabet for each letter in the set. Use each clue and its code to spell the answer. For example, E N O V B spells radio. In this exercise, there are four mystery letters identified by "?".

	Clue	Code	
1.	they stay out of the affairs of other nations	V F ? Y N G ? ? V F G	_____
2.	agreement to stop fighting	N E Z V F G V ? R	_____
3.	camp for political enemies	? ? ? ? R ? G E ? G V ? ? ? ? Z C	_____
4.	equipment for war	N E Z N Z R ? G F	_____
5.	mass murder of a people	T R ? ? ? V Q R	_____
6.	right to rule	Z N ? Q N G R	_____
7.	fighting in which armies have dug themselves into the ground	G E R ? ? U J N E S N E	_____

(continued)

USING VOCABULARY, cont.

	Clue	Code	
8.	uniting small farms into large, government-controlled ones	? ? Y Y R ? G V I V M N G V ? ?	_____
9.	sharp down-turn in the economy	Q R C E R F F V B ?	_____
10.	Nazi plan to kill the Jews of Europe	U ? Y ? ? ? H F G	_____
11.	hooked black cross	F J N F G V X N	_____
12.	person with absolute authority	Q V ? G N G B E	_____
13.	lightning war	? Y V G M X E V R T	_____
14.	manufacture of basic materials and machines	U R N I L V ? O H F G E L	_____

IMPORTANT WORLD EVENTS: 1900-1945

In the left column is a list of dates. Fill in the blanks next to the dates in the left column with the letters of important events listed in the right column.

Early 1900s

1914 _____

1917 _____

1918 _____

In the 1920s

1922 _____

1929 _____

In the 1930s

1931 _____

1933 _____

In the 1940s

1941 _____

1943 _____

1945 _____

A. U.S. declared war on Germany in retaliation for sinking civilian ships.

B. The Soviet Union was formed and controlled by Communist party.

C. Red Army surrounded German forces at Stalingrad.

D. An armistice was signed. World War I was over.

E. Atomic bomb dropped on Hiroshima, Japan.

F. World War I began in Europe.

G. Japan waged a surprise attack on Pearl Harbor. The U.S. enters WWII.

H. An economic depression affects the world.

I. Japan invaded mainland China.

J. Adolf Hitler became chancellor of Germany.

WORKING WITH MAPS

The map below contains the boundaries of post-World War II Europe. Use the atlas section in your text to complete this activity.

1. *Label the following bodies of water: Mediterranean Sea, Atlantic Ocean, Black Sea, and Baltic Sea.*

2. *Locate and label the following countries immediately following World War II: Poland, East Germany, West Germany, France, Spain, Portugal, Romania, Bulgaria, Greece, Turkey, Albania, Yugoslavia, Italy, Hungary, Austria, Switzerland, Czechoslovakia, Union of Soviet Socialist Republics, Finland, Sweden, Norway, Denmark, Netherlands, Belgium, United Kingdom, and Ireland.*

The Cold War Era (1945-1989)

Chapter 38

FOCUS ON IDEAS

Three topics are given below for Chapter 38. Write a paragraph about each topic.

An Uneasy Peace

1. _____

_____

_____

_____

_____

_____

Communist Powers

2. _____

_____

_____

_____

_____

_____

Developing Nations

3. _____

_____

_____

_____

_____

_____

USING VOCABULARY

Fill in the squares by spelling out the terms given in the clues below.

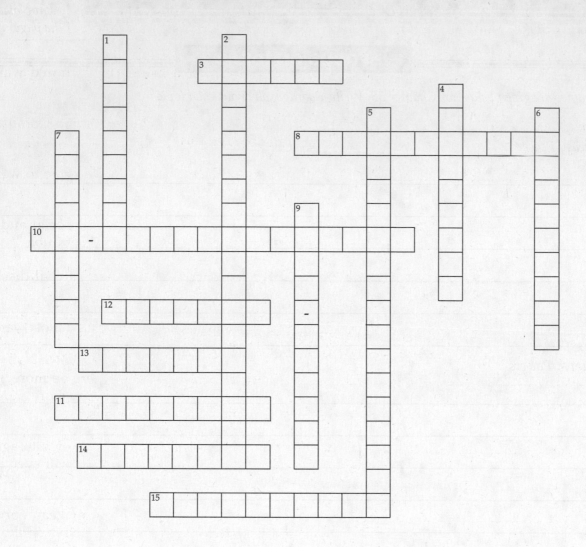

ACROSS

3. removal of undesirable members
8. means Soviet restructuring
10. attack on Stalin's policies
11. means closed off
12. way to carry supplies by airplane
13. state of hostilities without fighting
14. openness in the former Soviet Union
15. peasants who farm for rich landowners in Latin America

DOWN

1. crops sold in world markets
2. produce only enough for their own families
4. dividing the land of a country
5. countries with little industry and many poor, uneducated land workers
6. property is mostly privately owned
7. large ranches in Latin America
9. people who stick to rules

WHO MIGHT HAVE SAID...

Read the imaginary quotations below and decide which twentieth-century notable person might have made the statement. Write their names on the lines provided. Suggested leaders are listed at the bottom of the page.

1. _____   "No, this war will remain a limited war. No atomic weapons!"

2. _____   "North Vietnam shall exist as a Communist nation, and I shall lead."

3. _____   "I wish all Americans could be here to walk on the moon with me."

4. _____   "I promise free elections, and social and economic improvements throughout Cuba."

5. _____   "We will succeed if we practice civil disobedience in every needed situation."

6. _____   "In three years, I have conquered most warlords with words or with weapons."

7. _____   "Let our people live! Let there be more apartment housing, more clothing, more automobiles, and more television sets."

8. _____   "We will invest additional money into agricultural and consumer goods. We will even allow some private industry again."

9. _____   "Surely our program, the Great Leap Forward, will increase industrial production in the People's Republic of China."

10. _____   "The Chinese economy will improve under the Four Modernizations."

11. _____   "South Africa must end apartheid."

Fidel Castro	Mikhail S. Gorbachev	Chiang K'ai-shek	Harry S Truman
Nelson Mandela	Ho Chi Minh	Neil Armstrong	Mao Zedong
Mohandas Gandhi	Deng Xiaoping	Nikita Khrushchev	

WORKING WITH MAPS

Study the map to answer the questions below. Write your answers on the lines provided. You may need to use your textbook.

ASIA 1985

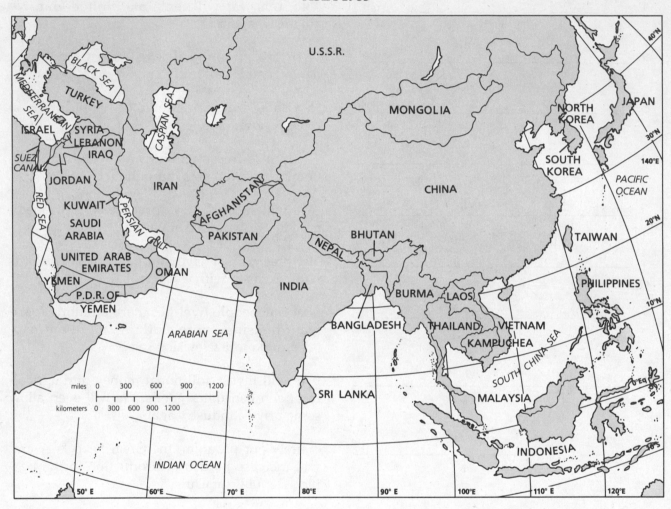

1. Approximately how many miles (kilometers) is Korea from the north to the south?

   miles _____ kilometers _____ From the east to the west? miles _____ kilometers _____

2. What is the distance in miles (kilometers) from the mainland of China to the island of Taiwan?

   miles _____ kilometers _____

3. In what two countries has the United States of America waged limited wars?

   _____

4. What countries bordered China? _____

   _____

BEING CREATIVE: Design Your Own Postcard

Imagine that you are visiting a developing country of the world. Below is the typical space of a postcard that you might send to a friend back home. Decide what country you are visiting. For A, draw a possible scene of what you might see on the trip. For B, write a message to a friend explaining the scene on the postcard. Along with your message, draw a stamp that might tell one more facts about the country.

A.

B.

Name _____ Date _____ Class _____

USING AN ELECTRONIC SPREADSHEET

All spreadsheets follow a basic design. Fill in the blanks below to help you identify the terms used in an electronic spreadsheet. Use the words in the box. Textbook page 636 will help you complete the page.

2B + 2C + 2D

	A	B	C	D	E
1					TOTAL
2					
3					
4					
5					
6					
7					
8					
9					
10					

1. _____ a vertical designation to store data

2. _____ a horizontal designation to store data

3. _____ intersection of a row and a column

4. _____ example of a label given to a cell's position

5. _____ a mathematical equation that the computer uses to do calculations

6. _____ term computer uses to display answer to calculations

B4	row	total	cell	standard formula	column

The World Since 1989

FOCUS ON IDEAS

Three topics are given below for Chapter 39. Write a paragraph about each topic.

The End of the Cold War

1. _____
   _____
   _____
   _____
   _____
   _____
   _____

World Challenges

2. _____
   _____
   _____
   _____
   _____
   _____
   _____

The World Today

3. _____
   _____
   _____
   _____
   _____
   _____
   _____

USING VOCABULARY   **Chapter 39**

Unscramble the letters in the first column to spell out the term being described in the second column. Then, write the unscrambled word in the third column.

tahdareip	forced separation of races	_ _ _ _ _ _ _ _ _
oupc	forced takeover	_ _ _ _
oamnuutoso	self-governing	_ _ _ _ _ _ _ _ _ _
gsaoigrsen	war-like acts	_ _ _ _ _ _ _ _ _
ernoegivs	self-governing nations	_ _ _ _ _ _ _ _
aitdanfi	Palestinian uprising	_ _ _ _ _ _ _
oeru	common currency of the European Union countries	_ _ _ _
tiuhiartonara lrue	government in which one ruler or political party holds power	_ _ _ _ _ _ _ _ _ _ _ _ _ _ _ _ _
uofmr	meeting place	_ _ _ _ _
zeapivtir	allow citizens to have ownership of their economy	_ _ _ _ _ _ _ _ _
cmpasnied	epidemics spread over a wide region	_ _ _ _ _ _ _ _ _
rsortierm	violence to achieve a political objective	_ _ _ _ _ _ _ _ _
ereedagn tsoanni	countries that refuse to reduce war weapons	_ _ _ _ _ _ _ _ _ _ _ _ _
eheosguren fceetf	situation when carbon dioxide traps heat near earth's surface	_ _ _ _ _ _ _ _ _ _ _ _ _ _
durrfeemne	popular vote	_ _ _ _ _ _ _ _ _

Name _____ Date _____ Class _____

READING A DEMOGRAPHIC MAP

The demographic map on page 651 of your textbook shows information about the world's population. Use this map to create a bar graph of average population. Note the population density that exists over the majority of land of each continent. Show the approximate population as a bar for each continent on the graph below. Then answer the questions that follow.

Average Population
per sq. mile

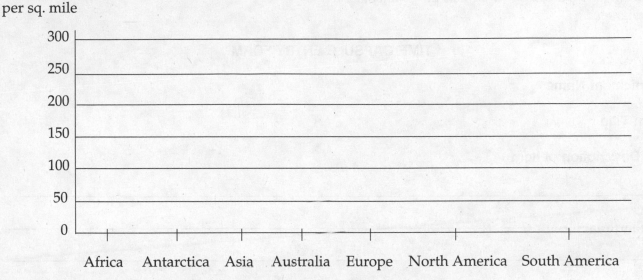

1. Which continent has the greatest population? _____

2. Which two continents have little or no population? _____

3. Which two continents would be most affected by a spreading, deadly disease?

   _____ Why? _____

4. Compare the population densities of North and South America. What similarities do you see?

   _____

   What differences are there?

   _____

   _____

Name _____ Date _____ Class _____

Imagine that you live in a world community that has decided to plant a time capsule to be opened 50 years in the future. The time capsule team has said items to be enclosed should tell future citizens about your present life—food, clothing, shelter, religions, government, education, health care, transportation, family groupings, art, literature, entertainment, electronic communication industry, food production, money system, and electronic commerce.

Below is a form to be completed for each possible time capsule item. The time capsule team will determine the items to be enclosed based on the form's information. Part A is a written explanation of why you have selected the item. Part B is space to draw how the item will look.

TIME CAPSULE ENTRY FORM

Participant Name

Item Title

A. Description of Item

_____

_____

_____

_____

_____

_____

B. Draw a sketch to show the item. Include dimensions if necessary.

Name _____ Date _____ Class _____

Geography and History

WORLD CHALLENGES

Use textbook pages 652–662 to complete the page.

A. Fill in the blanks to complete a comparison chart on dramatic world challenges that have arisen in the late 20th century.

WORLD CHALLENGES	PLACE IN WORLD	OUTCOME
Invasion of oil-rich Kuwait by Iraqi dictator		Coalition forces attacked Iraq—the Gulf War
	Balkan nations	NATO, with UN backing, intervened; a shaky peace
Kosovar Liberation Army (KLA) called for Kosovo's independence; ethnic cleansing in Albania		Kosovo, a Serbian province under UN supervision
	Middle Eastern countries	Israel and Palestine sign treaty in 1993. Israel and Jordan sign in 1994. Israel and Syria begin talks in December 1999.
Possible peace between Catholics and Protestants in Ireland	Northern Ireland	
New Chinese leader, Jiang Zemin, oversees change		Returns to China; United States urges restraint on both sides and enters trade talks
Trouble in Indonesia—decrease of people's freedom	17,000 islands stretching from Malaysian Peninsula towards Australia	
Progress in Africa		Holds its second all-race democratic election in 1999

B. In the space provided, draw your own political cartoon that shows your opinion about one of the world challenges you listed above. Include a title and caption for your cartoon.

UNIT 12 AROUND THE WORLD

NUNAVUT

Complete a brief profile of Canada's largest and newest self-governing territory by filling in the blanks below. Use textbook pages 668-669 to complete the page.

COUNTRY PROFILE

NAME:

Nunavut means _____

CAPITAL:

Iqaluit is closest to what Canadian city? _____

FLAG:

Nunavut's territorial symbol is the _____, the pile of stones used by Inuit hunters to mark trails.

LOCATION:

Nunavut makes up nearly one-fifth of all Canadian land. More than one-half of it lies _____ of the Arctic Circle. It stretches across _____ time zones.

GEOGRAPHY:

Nunavut is carved out of the Northwest Territories. It is a sprawling region of _____, Arctic islands, and frozen _____. Animals outnumber _____ by 25 to 1.

CHALLENGES OF NUNAVUT:

Approximately 28 villages are _____, with only a few hundred people living in each one. _____ percent of the people are under the age of 25. Winters are very long, and much of the land is _____ frozen.

ROLE MODEL FOR ENTIRE WORLD:

For the first time in Canada's history, a _____ people had won control of their own government. The people of Nunavut have the right to send a territorial representative to the Canadian _____. The creation of Nunavut gives the Inuit, who make up 85 percent of the population, a chance to _____ their culture in the century ahead.